THE BAR EXAM
IN A NUTSHELL

By

SUZANNE DARROW-KLEINHAUS
Assistant Professor of Legal Methods
Touro College Jacob D. Fuchsberg Law Center

THOMSON

WEST

Mat # 40149072

Nutshell Series, In a Nutshell, the Nutshell Logo and West Group are trademarks registered in the U.S. Patent and Trademark Office.

© 2003 By West, a Thomson business
      610 Opperman Drive
      P.O. Box 64526
      St. Paul, MN 55164–0526
      1–800–328–9352

ISBN 0–314–14641–5

In memory of
our beloved Cindy

*

PREFACE AND ACKNOWLEDGMENTS

The bar exam looms large in the mind of every law student from the first day of law school and sometimes even before. But it need not. The bar exam is a practical exam that requires a practical approach. It's meant to test the candidate's basic competency to practice law—to see whether the law student has mastered the legal skills and general knowledge that a first year practicing attorney should possess.

Still, the bar exam is a challenge and the candidate cannot simply graduate law school and expect to pass without any additional preparation. But law school was also a challenge and presumably the candidate made it through or he or she would not be taking the bar exam. The truth is that law school prepares candidates for the bar by providing a solid foundation in the skills the bar exam seeks to test and in turning out an individual who knows how to handle the competing demands on his or her time, memory, and energy. When a student has learned how to learn the law, then bar passage is not an obstacle that cannot be overcome, but a requirement for entering the profession which must be met like any other.

First and always, my husband Murray. His love, support, encouragement, and meals have been constant throughout our marriage, and especially throughout the writing of this book. Our family would have starved long ago if it weren't for him.

I owe much to my daughter Meredith who believed in my ability to teach before I did, insisting that I was so much clearer and better at explaining how to write than any of her high school or college teachers that I should be the one who wrote her textbooks and taught her classes. She believed in me so strongly that she sent all of her friends to me for help. My sister, Jessica read the early drafts and made some great suggestions. Together we reminisced about our bar prep days and tried to come up with what we would have wanted to know to make the task even the slightest bit more tolerable. Many thanks to my parents, Bernice and Albert, who taught me so much, but especially my dad, who reminded me when I was tired and disheartened that I should never let go of my dream to teach and to write.

I am truly indebted to all of my teachers life long, including and particularly, my dear friends and mentors, Professors Michael D'Innocenzo and Ruth Prigozy. Their voices are now and for always in my head.

And of course, my students, for whom this book is intended and without whom it would not have been written. The development of "forensic IRAC' would not have been possible without their willingness to open up and let me into their thoughts.

My deepest appreciation to Touro College, Jacob D. Fuchsberg Law Center and especially Dean

Howard Glickstein and Vice Dean Gary Shaw for their unreserved support and unwavering commitment to our students.

———————

I've endeavored to make clear throughout the book that the candidate's best friends during this time are the Bar Examiners. Both the National Conference of Bar Examiners ("NCBE") and the state boards make numerous materials available to bar candidates.

The Multistate Bar Examination ("MBE") questions, the Multistate Essay Examination ("MEE") interrogatory, and excerpts from the Multistate Performance Tests ("MPT") have been reprinted by permission from the NCBE. Any attempt to create a useful manual for bar candidates would been impossible without these materials.

The MBE questions have been "Reprinted by Permission" from the following NCBE publications: Sample MBE February, 1991 (© 1991 by the National Conference of Bar Examiners), Sample MBE 1996 (© 1996 by the National Conference of Bar Examiners), Sample MBE III July,1998 (© 1998 by the National Conference of Bar Examiners) and the 2001 Information Booklet (© 2001 by the National Conference of Bar Examiners).

The MEE interrogatory has been "Reprinted by Permission" from the February, 2000 MEE (© 2000 by the National Conference of Bar Examiners).

The MPT excerpts have been "Reprinted by Permission" from Test 2 of the February 1997, MPT,

In re Hayworth and Wexler (© 1997 by the National Conference of Bar Examiners) and Test 2 of the July 1997, MPT, *State v. Devine* (© 1997 by the National Conference of Bar Examiners).

Like the NCBE, the individual state bar examiners make vital information available to its bar candidates. It's all right there on the internet and I made extensive use of this vital resource. I urge all candidates to do the same. Each jurisdiction administers the exam and determines its own policy with regard to the relative weight given to the scores for each component of the bar exam. As a result, it's the primary source for such basic information as application materials, test locations and accommodations, test dates, admissions issues, test topics, and more. Even more importantly, most jurisdictions include some examples of past exam questions and sample answers.

In addition to the National Conference of Bar Examiners, I wish to thank the bar examiners of New York, New Jersey, and Connecticut for permission to reprint bar examination materials. The reprinted essay selections and sample answers have all been downloaded from the states' web sites, in large part to illustrate the accessibility of these materials to bar candidates.

In New York, the Board of Law Examiners release answers which received scores superior to the average scale score awarded for the relevant essay. However, the Board is careful to make no representation as to the accuracy of the answers; they are simply considered above average responses.

Like New York, the bar examiners in New Jersey and Connecticut publish essay questions after each bar examination administration. In New Jersey, the Board publishes actual answers from candidates that it considers to be exceptional although they are not intended as model answers. The State of Connecticut publishes seven sample answers for each essay question, providing the applicant with an opportunity to see a range of scores. Connecticut's bar examiners identify the scoring system and the candidate can read what was considered a "much below average" response as opposed to a "much above average" response, and everything in between.

A regularly updated list of each jurisdiction's bar admission office phone number and address can be found at www.ncbex.org, the NCBE's official website.

SUZANNE DARROW-KLEINHAUS
BELLMORE, NEW YORK

June 2003

*

OUTLINE

THE BAR EXAM
IN A NUTSHELL

*

CHAPTER 1

ABOUT THE BAR EXAM

A. WHY SHOULD YOU LISTEN TO ME?

If you're like other bar candidates, you've been bombarded with lots of well-meaning advice on how to prepare for the bar exam. You may even have paid thousands of dollars for this advice. So what could another so-called "bar expert" possibly have to tell you that is not already to be found somewhere in the pile of materials growing like Mount Vesuvius on the side of your bed? Simple: I can tell you what you need to know to make all this guidance work for you and not simply overwhelm you. I can share with you what I have learned in the past five years from working with classmates, students, and other bar candidates who failed the bar exam multiple times and then passed after we had worked together. I can spare you what they went through trying to figure out what the exam was all about. Then you can pass the bar exam the first time you take it.

I sat for the bar exam five years ago. The experience is fresh in my mind—vividly so—as it remains for all of us who take the bar. I promise that you'll never forget the struggle of studying for and taking the bar exam; I also promise that you'll never forget the moment of joy and exhilaration when you learn that you've passed. And that is what this book is all about—getting you to that moment.

I never thought I would make the bar exam some kind of personal calling. I was just happy that it was behind me and I could pack away my flash cards, notebooks, and the ton of study materials I had accumulated. But my happiness was short-lived when I learned that my best friends had not passed with me. I was shocked: I knew my friends had studied long hours, like me. I knew that they had gone to all the bar review classes and had taken copious notes, like me. I knew that they had followed the suggested study outlines and prepared sample essays, like me. So why the different result? I wanted to do something—anything—to help.

I offered to study with them. I had been a good student in law school and one of my essays had been selected as a sample answer in New York. I felt I had something of value to offer. We started to meet weekly at my house and as we sat around the kitchen table, working through essay questions and multiple choice questions together, I was able to see how they approached the problems. From that first afternoon, it became clear to me that while we had gone to law school together, taken exams together, and had even taken the same bar review course together, we went about the process of analyzing and answering the questions very differently. I used IRAC and they didn't. It never occurred to me that using IRAC, the method of legal analysis taught to all law students from the very first day of law school, would make the difference between passing and failing, but it did, and as I was soon to learn, it always makes the difference.

B. YOU MEAN THAT IRAC IS THE SECRET?

As I continued to work with more and more students, it became increasingly clear that the secret to passing the bar exam, if there was a secret at all, was not the amount of time spent in study but the nature of that study and the diligent application of IRAC analysis to all problems, essay and short answer alike. The key to getting multiple choice questions correct and high essay scores was finding the issue in each of the questions and working from there. This sounds a lot easier and a lot harder than it is so a little explanation is in order.

It's easier because you're already acquainted with IRAC: the acronym for the familiar "Issue, Rule, Application, Conclusion" structure of legal analysis. It's more difficult because you're probably not familiar enough with it to use it consistently and correctly to reason through objective, short answer questions as well as essay questions where you are given only a general question and must identify the narrow issue in controversy for yourself. Typically, your understanding of IRAC is limited to the form your professors wanted you to use to write an essay exam. But IRAC is more than a form: it is the essence and structure of all legal reasoning.

The questions on the bar exam and its individual sections are designed to test the fundamental analytical skills you learned in law school together with your mastery of legal principles and basic knowledge of core substance. Over and over again, in one format or another, you'll be given a set of facts and must know enough law to find the legal problem. Your ability to find the legal question in the facts is the single most important element in the analysis because you need to know enough law to find the issue. But you must do more than just find the issue: you must identify it and clearly articulate it, either to yourself for the multiple choice questions or in writing for the essays, before you can go on and correctly answer the question or write an essay that gets you the necessary points.

Your ability to conscientiously and consistently apply IRAC analysis to all the questions will make the difference between passing and failing. While there are certainly a number of other factors involved in the equation, and I will discuss them in the course of this book, I've learned that the one common thread linking all the unsuccessful candidates I've worked with was their failure to use IRAC to analyze the questions. It was not enough that they had mastered the substantive rules of law: they needed to know when a particular rule was implicated by the facts. This was the connection between them and what they had been missing. By failing to identify the issue, they failed to recognize when a particular rule was in controversy. Then it didn't matter whether they knew the rule or not.

They never got to apply it because they didn't see the issue. The good news is that once these students integrated IRAC analysis into the course and method of their study, they went on to pass the exam.

C. THE ELEMENTS OF SUCCESS

After hundreds of hours of working with students to prepare for the bar exam, I've managed to identify the essential elements required for success. They are really quite simple and make a great deal of sense because they are based on the skills the bar examiners seek to test on the exam.

These skills include:

- problem solving,
- identifying and formulating legal issues,
- organizing information,
- separating relevant from irrelevant facts,
- communicating effectively in writing, and
- managing time efficiently to complete an assignment.

The problem is that these are practical skills and students spend most if not all of their bar prep time studying only substantive law. Success on the bar exam requires mastery of both.

1. Not Just Memorization But Application

Your bar review course will provide all the substantive law you need to know to pass the exam. Such courses are carefully constructed to give you the black letter law in all the areas of law tested in your jurisdiction. When you think about it, this is a prodigious effort and best left to the professionals. Don't try to do this on your own.

Still, you'll need to practice the theoretical rule of law in the practical context of how it will be tested. It is not enough to memorize elements and rules without some idea of how they will be tested. Given the tremendous amount of material you'll cover in your bar review classes, the volume of notes you'll take, and the number of outlines you'll be given, you can easily get caught up in spending all your time reviewing this stuff and never make it to the next step. The tendency is for precious study time to slip away without spending adequate time practicing the rules as well as memorizing them. While your bar review course will provide a study schedule that factors in practice time with essay and multiple choice questions, my experience has shown that it is not enough for most students. Just imagine going to take your road test and never doing more than read the driver's manual and drive the car around the block a few times. Well, going into the bar exam without doing hundreds (yes, I said "hundreds") of multiple choice questions and a significant number of essays will leave you in the same place: without the license you want.

An example from a past Multistate Bar Exam ("MBE") question illustrates this point nicely.

Peavey was walking peacefully along a public street when he encountered Dorwin, whom he had never seen before. Without provocation or warning, Dorwin picked up a rock and struck Peavey with it. It was later established that Dorwin was mentally ill and suffered recurrent hallucinations.

If Peavey asserts a claim against Dorwin based on battery, which of the following, if supported by evidence, will be Dorwin's best defense?

    A.   Dorwin did not understand that his act was wrongful.

    B.   Dorwin did not desire to cause harm to Peavey.

    C.   Dorwin did not know that he was striking a person.

    D.   Dorwin thought Peavey was about to attack him.

You could spend hours studying your notes on intentional torts, "know" the elements of a battery, and still answer this question incorrectly if you're unfamiliar with the way the elements are tested on the bar exam. If you're like most law students, you learned the elements of the intentional torts in a rather straightforward manner: you read cases, identified the elements in class discussions, memorized them, and recited them back on the final in the context of an essay.

You can see that the bar exam takes a different approach. Your analysis begins with the basic definition of a battery, but that's only your first step. Then you have to analyze each element with respect to the legal issue posed in the hypothetical. If you fail to identify the issue or miss the signal words in the question, you'll arrive at an incorrect answer choice even though you could probably recite the elements of a battery in your sleep!

Typically, I ask a student to answer this question when we begin working together and use it as a kind of "legal" Rorschach test to evaluate the student's substantive knowledge and analytical skills. I am not surprised when the majority of students choose an incorrect answer. For example, one student selected Answer Choice B, explaining that because a battery is the intentional, harmful or offensive touching of another, if Dorwin did not intend to cause harm, then he could not have committed a battery. "Yes," I replied, "but did Dorwin have to intend harm to commit a battery?" The student thought about it and realized that Dorwin need not have intended harm to be found liable in battery.

Not surprisingly, Choice B was the most popular student answer choice. Why? Because if you read the question quickly and scan the answer choices, you jump to Choice B because it contains the familiar battery language: "desire to cause harm."

Choice B was followed closely by Choice A in student popularity. Once again, Choice A reflects a student's tendency to react to answer choices instead of applying the elements mechanically to the issue in the question. Here, the student explained his answer choice as follows: if Dorwin didn't understand his act to be wrongful, then it couldn't have been "intentional." Just as in Answer Choice B, this reasoning is flawed because the intent element of battery is satisfied not only when the actor intends harmful or wrongful behavior, but if he acts with purpose or knowledge to a "substantial certainty." Here, Dorwin need not have understood his act to be wrongful to have formed the requisite intent: he need only know what would be the likely consequence of striking Peavey with a rock. Consequently, only Choice C completely negates the intent element: if Dorwin had no idea (no "knowledge") he was striking a person, then he could not have formed the requisite intent to do the act.

A number of students selected Choice D. Interestingly, there were two lines of incorrect reasoning to support this answer choice! In one instance, the rationale was that self-defense would be a valid justification to excuse Dorwin's act. "Where in the facts do you find any basis to believe that Peavey was about to attack Dorwin?" I asked. Each student shook his or her head: "Nowhere," each reluctantly conceded. Once again, students had reacted to an answer choice without analyzing it within the factual context of the problem. If they had, they would have realized that there were no facts in the question to lead Dorwin to believe Peavey was about to attack him. In fact, careful reading of the problem would have ruled this answer choice out completely because the first words in the question tell us that "Peavey was walking peacefully" and it was "without provocation or warning, [that] Dorwin picked up a rock." How much clearer could the bar examiners have been? This leads us to Rule One for multiple choice questions: do not assume facts and do not select answer choices that have no basis in the facts of the problem unless a modifier like "unless" or "if" in the answer choice supplies the needed additional facts.

The other line of reasoning relied on the Mc'Naughton rule regarding the insanity defense to a criminal act. The problem, however, is that this was not a criminal prosecution and candidates who arrived at this conclusion did so by failing to read the facts carefully. We are told in the question stem that "Peavey asserts a claim against Dorwin based on battery" which must mean that it is a claim in "civil" battery; if it had been a criminal battery, then the state would have initiated the action.

I've spent a lot of time with you on this problem because it so accurately reflects the nature of an MBE question. As you can see, it seeks to test your true understanding of a subject and not just your ability to memorize. The problem itself comes from the famous tort case, *Garratt v. Dailey*. Remember Brian Dailey, the little five-year old who pulled the lawn chair from under the plaintiff as she was about to sit down? As the court stated in *Garratt*, "a battery would be established if, in addition to plaintiff's fall, it was proved that, when Brian moved the chair, he knew with substantial certainty that the plaintiff would attempt to sit down where the chair had been.... [t]he mere absence of any intent to injure the plaintiff or to play a prank on her or to embarrass her, or to commit an assault and battery on her would not absolve him from liability if, in fact, he had such knowledge." 46 Wash.2d 197, 279 P.2d 1091 (1955). You can see how applying this definition of intent makes Choice C the correct response. If Dorwin did not know that he was striking a person, then he could not have committed a wrongful act.

It should be clear from this example how you must reason through an MBE question using IRAC or you'll respond incorrectly to a relatively simple torts question. In each case, you must identify the main issue in the question and then address the mini-issues raised in the answer choices. This requires that you ask yourself what's going on in the problem. Here, you're asked to solve a problem by finding Dorwin's best defense. To do this, you'll have to identify the answer choice which prevents the plaintiff from prevailing. This requires that you identify the elements of the plaintiff's cause of action, determine which defense would be strongest (negates that element), and choose an answer which most closely provides a basis for overcoming that obstacle. When you begin doing MBE questions, this thought process will require effort and a mechanical application of the steps; with sufficient practice, you'll run through these steps automatically.

2.   What This Book Will Do For You

This book will show you how to balance the need for memorization with the need for application. Since you must do both to succeed on the exam, this book will tell you how to effectively manage your time and the materials so that you can do both. By now you must realize that this book won't tell you that it is enough for you to attend all of your bar review sessions and simply memorize rules of law. It also won't tell you to spend all of your time reviewing your notes and making index cards. And it surely won't tell you to become a robot and place yourself in the hands of others to prepare for what might well be the most important test of your life.

The bar exam requires that you think like a lawyer—perhaps for the very first time. Therefore, this book will show you how to rely on your training to respond to questions with an orderly thought process instead of panicking when you come cross an unfamiliar question. It will teach you how to internalize the thought process required to succeed and show you how to perform "forensic IRAC" on your own thought process so you can identify the flaws in your legal reasoning and correct them.

Further, this book will show you how to put together an individualized study program that works for you because it works from your strengths while recognizing your weaknesses. It will de-construct the bar exam and separate it into its component parts. By conquering the parts, you master the whole.

And finally, this book will teach you how to act under pressure. When you study for the bar exam, you are facing one of the most stressful periods of your life. You may be consumed with thoughts of "what if": what if I fail; what if I have to do this again; what if I don't get the job that I want; what if I disappoint my family, my friends, my teachers, myself. These are very normal fears: we all share them. In fact, a certain level of anxiety is a good thing but too much prevents you from doing your job. And you must be able to do your job of studying the law. You can't afford to lose control because of the pressure. Hemingway referred to it as having "grace under pressure." He wrote about the beauty and purity of line of the bull fighter in the ring facing the bull. The bull fighter's ability to remain focused and in control allowed him to control the bull and hence the outcome of the contest. You need to do the same in your arena.

CHAPTER 2

PLANNING FOR THE EVENT

A. THE NEED FOR PREPARATION

Studying for the bar exam is an experience unlike any other. Preparing for the bar exam isn't easy, enjoyable, or anything less than the tremendous pain that it is. But it is doable and countless others before you have done it and you'll do it too. And you should plan on doing it only once. That is the point of this book. If you put in the time and effort required for the period involved, then it will be behind you forever—unless you choose to take the bar exam in another jurisdiction. But then it will be your choice, not the bar examiners.

Taking the bar exam is like running a marathon. And you need to prepare the same way. But don't jump to any conclusions about your author—she has never run a marathon and never intends to do so. But she is married to a marathon runner and she sees the training and discipline and planning that precedes marathon day. Preparing for the bar exam is very similar—you too must be in top physical and mental form to compete successfully in what amounts to a triathalon.

Just think about it. You're facing two days (maybe three in some jurisdictions or if you're taking the bar exam in two jurisdictions) of intense, focused concentration. This means that you must be able to shift analytically from a consideration of future interests, to third-party interests, to a criminal defendant's standing to assert a fourth amendment violation, and so on to 97 other such scenarios in the span of three hours. And after a short break, you need to do it all again for another three hours. The bar exam is nothing short of a test of your mental and physical endurance as well as a test of your legal knowledge and skills.

B. A PRACTICAL EXAM REQUIRES A PRACTICAL APPROACH

Admittedly, this is a challenge. But so was law school and you made it through or you wouldn't be here now. The good news is that law school prepared you for this exam. You've already spent three years, maybe four if you were a part-time student, training for this event. What's eight more weeks?

If you listen to what bar examiners have to say (and you really should pay attention to them because they write and score the exam), the bar exam is designed to test your basic competency to practice law. It's meant to see whether you've mastered the legal skills and general knowledge that a first year practicing attorney should possess. In short, the bar exam seeks to test the sum total of your lawyering skills. Most candidates, however, tend to overlook the practical nature of the exam and focus solely on memorizing as much black letter law as possible.

While it is absolutely essential that you learn black letter law, you must also sharpen your basic analytical, reading, and writing skills. You can easily fall into the trap of devoting all your time and energy to memorizing rules without ever developing your practical sense of how the law works. You'll be amazed at how many answers to questions depend as much on your understanding of general legal principles as on your knowledge of specific rules. To borrow a cliche, don't be so busy looking at the trees that you forget about the forest.

Once again, a past Multistate question illustrates this point nicely.

Dawson was charged with felony murder because of his involvement in a bank robbery. The evidence at trial disclosed that Smith invited Dawson to go for a ride in his new car, and after a while asked Dawson to drive. As Smith and Dawson drove around town, Smith explained to Dawson that he planned to rob the bank and that he needed Dawson to drive the getaway car. Dawson agreed to drive to the bank and to wait outside while Smith went in to rob it. As they approached the bank, Dawson began to regret his agreement to help with the robbery. Once there, Smith got out of the car. As Smith went out of sight inside the bank, Dawson drove away and went home. Inside the bank, Smith killed a bank guard who tried to prevent him from leaving with the money. Smith ran outside and, finding that his car and Dawson were gone, ran down an alley. He was apprehended a few blocks away. Dawson later turned himself in after hearing on the radio that Smith killed the guard.

The jurisdiction has a death penalty that applies to felony murder. Consistent with the law and the Constitution, the jury may convict Dawson of:

(A) Felony murder and impose the death penalty.

(B) Felony murder but not impose the death penalty.

(C) Bank robbery only.

(D) No crime.

I'll be the first to admit that I answered this question incorrectly. I was so busy identifying and applying the elements of felony murder, and the possible defenses, that I completely failed to consider the Eighth Amendment's prohibition against "cruel and unusual punishments." The correct response is Choice B. A thoughtful reading of the language in the question stem should have made me pause and consider what limits the Constitution places on a criminal conviction. The question is not always about a direct application of a particular rule but an appreciation and understanding of the general principles of law and how they impact the rules. Strict memorization won't help you here but the sum and substance of your legal education will.

C. RELY ON YOUR LEGAL TRAINING

Lawyers are trained to solve problems and now you're a lawyer. Typically, the problems to be solved will be your clients', but in this case you're the client. Your first priority is to pass the bar exam. You are going to use the problem-solving skills you've learned as a lawyer to help yourself.

We've already identified the exam as a practical exam. This means that you'll be practical too and take a practical approach. That's what you'd do for a client. First, you'd consider your client's position in terms of the merits of the case, i.e., its strengths and weaknesses. Second, you'd identify the possible courses of action you could take based on the nature of the case. Well, you're going to do the same thing for yourself. You're going to assess your strengths and weaknesses in terms of the skills tested on the exam and then you're going to structure your study program accordingly.

Your plan should account for the following:

- Selecting the right bar review course for the way that you learn

- Getting your "house in order" so that you have a clear head to study

- Identifying the basic skills tested on the exam

D. SELECTING THE RIGHT BAR RE-VIEW COURSE

No one does it alone. Do not even attempt to do so. The commercial bar review course is essential to your success because it will provide all the law you need to know in a structured, cohesive package. These courses serve another important function as well: they provide much needed emotional guidance

and support as you go through the tedious preparation period. They provide a structured study envi-
ronment and insure that you will cover all the law
necessary to succeed on the exam.

Your task is to select the course best suited to
how you learn. Do you learn by listening? By writing? By a combination of both? Can you study on
my own or do you need a daily regimen of classes
and assignments? While most law students have
made the commitment to a bar review course before
the end of their legal education, it is not too late
and you should strongly consider choosing one to
guide you now. Make some phone calls, ask questions, and review the materials. Assess your individual learning style and make a choice. You'll be glad
you did.

E. GETTING   YOUR   "HOUSE   IN ORDER"

1. Setting Aside the Time

This is an important step in your study plan and
one that is easily overlooked. Nobody really tells
you about this kind of stuff but it's a vital part of
the process. You must plan ahead to give yourself
enough study time. The optimum period would be
eight weeks of uninterrupted, concentrated study
time but I know that for some of you there's no way
to free yourself from pressing family, financial, and
work obligations to set aside this amount of time.
Certainly, candidates have passed the bar exam
while relying on less study time. But the stakes are

high and you want to do everything in your power to maximize the likelihood that you'll pass the first time around. To a large extent, success on the bar exam is a function of actual time spent in concentrated study. You need the time to focus solely on the law so that your head will be filled with law on bar day.

Also, you need to be free from worry in order to study effectively. This sounds funny—free from worry—when all you're going to do is worry about the exam, but I mean free from the basic worries of money, family obligations, living arrangements, and the countless other demands on your time and attention. It's hard to memorize the elements of crimes and learn the Rule Against Perpetuities when you're worrying about paying the rent or finding someone to watch little Adam and Ashley while you're taking the exam. These major life considerations must be addressed as early as possible so that you won't be distracted when you need to concentrate. There will always be life's little emergencies that come up along the way so if you've done your best to eliminate the major ones, you'll be able to deal with the unexpected ones as they arise and minimize their impact on your studies.

I would strongly recommend that you plan ahead for the time you'll need to study. If money is a concern, think about taking a loan to cover your basic needs during this time. If you must work, consider taking all of your available vacation time and sick time in the weeks prior to the exam. Give yourself as much time as you possibly can. If you consider the alternatives (as a true lawyer would do), you'll realize that the sooner you pass the bar, the sooner you get your license, the sooner you can practice law, and the sooner you can earn some money.

Also, consider asking friends and relatives to help you. Now is no time to be a martyr and insist on doing everything yourself. Let others help you. They can assist in a variety of ways, making them feel useful and a part of the process. They can baby sit; they can prepare meals and run errands. But most importantly, they can be understanding of your situation. You'll need the people in your life to realize how critical this time is for you and that you'll not be available to them in the same way you may have been in the past. If you prepare your family and friends for your unavailability during this time, they will be more understanding when you have to refuse invitations because you have to study. Take heart. This doesn't last forever!

2.   Remember Your Health

Now is the time to see to your basic medical needs. Have a routine checkup. Take vitamins, exercise, get enough sleep, and watch what you eat. While now is not the time to go on a killer diet or give up smoking, you must take care of your basic health. You can put off any promises to quit smoking and give up chocolate until after the bar exam.

Now is not the time to add any more stress to your life!

Have your vision checked. While you read a lot during law school, you'll be pushing it to the limit during bar review. You want to make sure that you're using the right prescription. Also, go to the dentist. Don't wait. Toothaches don't go away. They get worse and you can't study when you're in pain.

I realize that most of these suggestions are just plain common sense. But I've seen some very smart people lose all perspective and do some very foolish things during this time.

3.   Some Final Checks

Now a word or two about the basics. Make sure your application is in on time. You don't want any last minute hassles in this area. Also, if you require special accommodations, make the arrangements early, rather than late.

Similarly, if you require hotel reservations, make them now. Don't wait until the last possible minute. As test day approaches, the last thing you need to think about is where you're staying or how you'll get to the test site. If you'll be traveling to the test, plan a trial run before the actual event. Know exactly where you're going and how long it will take to get there. Leave nothing to chance.

That brings us to the final issue of the test location itself. I firmly believe that there is nothing more frightening than the unknown. That's why I insist on practicing the types of questions you're going to see on the exam. It eliminates the surprise on test day. Therefore, I also insist on checking out the test site itself. You need to know what to expect. Will it be a big room? Will it be noisy? Will there be distractions? Will there be somewhere for you to go on your lunch break? Will you need to bring all of your own food? I worked with one student who was so psyched out by having to take the exam in a large conference center with over 5000 other students that she requested another location from the state's bar examiners. They were able to accommodate her request and she took the exam at a less populated site where she felt considerably more at ease.

I'm sure you can think of more questions. The best source for answers, of course, is your bar review course. It's familiar with the site in your area. Some courses even include practice exams in the test location. If you have this opportunity, grab it. Not only will it give you the much needed experience of sitting through the exam, it simulates exam conditions. You just don't get the same experience by taking a practice exam at the kitchen table.

Finally, you can ask others who have taken the exam. I'm sure you can think of a few classmates who graduated before you and have sat for the bar. Just remember to ask someone who has taken the exam rather recently. You want "current sense impressions," not old "war stories."

F. IDENTIFYING THE BASIC SKILLS TESTED ON THE EXAM

An effective study plan will incorporate skills practice as well as substantive review. By identifying the basic skills that the bar seeks to test, you can target your study efforts. Depending on your individual strengths and weaknesses, you will want to allocate your study time accordingly.

1. IRAC

First, you must be able to use the process of issue analysis to solve questions of law. You must apply IRAC to solve multiple choice questions, you must use IRAC to write your essay answers, and if your jurisdiction includes the Multistate Performance Test ("MPT"), you must use a modified form of IRAC to address the MPT problem.

If you know that you were weak in this area, then you need to factor in study time to practice and refine your IRAC skills. How do you know if you were weak in this area? One sure way is to recall the comments you received on your law school exams. Did your professors write such comments as "weak in application," "sketchy on the law," "missed the issue," or "unfocused analysis?" If so, what they really meant was that you failed to use IRAC appropriately to organize and write your analysis.

We're going to cure this problem. As we proceed through the parts of the exam, I will show you how to perform "forensic IRAC" on your own thought and writing process so you can identify the flaws in your legal analysis and correct them. By the time bar day arrives, the process of issue analysis to solve questions of law will be second nature to you.

2.   Reading Comprehension

Second, you must read actively and carefully and understand what you read. Note that I said "actively" and not "quickly." While the bar exam is a difficult exam in large part because of the time constraints, it is not so much a test of your ability to read rapidly, as it is a test of your ability to understand what you read. Reading "right" means that you'll find the issue in the question, that you'll identify the key words in the multiple choice questions, and that you'll follow directions to address only the problem that is asked of you.

Once again, if you know that you are an exceedingly slow reader, tend to misread, or consistently make mistakes in answering questions because you're a careless reader, you'll need to learn to read right. You'll practice reading questions from released bar exams and hone your reading skills by gaining familiarity with the language and structure of bar questions. There is a pattern and consistency to the length of essay questions and the structure, tone, and organization of multiple choice questions. You can become a careful and effective reader for the purposes of the bar exam and the subsequent practice of law.

3.   The Language of the Law

Third, you must **sound** like a lawyer in your essays. Good communications skills are essential for an attorney. Because the bar examiners don't get to meet with each of you individually and hear you argue orally, they must rely on the image you convey on paper. Think of your essays as dialogues with the bar examiners. You want to convince the grader who reads your essay that you're ready to take your place in the profession by sounding as if you're already there. This is your opportunity to show the grader that you're ready to meet with clients and address the court.

The use of legal terminology in your essays is essential. You have just completed several years acquiring a legal education where you must have read hundreds of cases. The language of Holmes, Cardozo, Brennan, and Blackmun should have made some impression on you. While your goal is not to impress the grader with your legal and literary brilliance, it is to provide a "scintilla of evidence" that you've read cases and can write a legal analysis using the language of the law.

CHAPTER 3

STUDYING FOR THE BAR EXAM

A. UNDERSTANDING THE PROCESS

I'm going to assume that you've followed my advice and selected a bar review course. I'm also going to assume that you're like the rest of us and after you've completed your first week of the course, you're in a panic because:

(A) you're feeling overwhelmed

(B) you're afraid that you're never going to be able to learn it all

(C) you're scared that you're going to fail

(D) all of the above

These feelings are absolutely normal. There would be something wrong with you if you didn't have them. There is a real basis to your anxiety. You have a lot of black letter law to learn and your future is riding on the outcome. Allow yourself to feel anxious but don't let yourself panic. Some anxiety is good and serves a purpose because it motivates you to work. Panic, on the other hand, only eats up valuable time by taking you away from your studies. Instead, you're going to accept the fact that the next two months will be something of an

27

emotional roller coaster and then you're going to get on with the business of studying.

B. DEFINE YOUR INDIVIDUAL STUDY PLAN

Even a couple of bar review sessions should have shown you that there's a big difference between studying for law school exams and studying for the bar exam. First, there is just so much more you're required to know at one time. For example, New Jersey pretty much relies on the basic Multistate subjects for its essays, but if you're sitting for the New York bar, add another 15 or so subjects to that list. Individual state requirements vary but any way you look at it, you're responsible for a wide range of material.

Second, in law school, exams were spread out over a period of time and the maximum number of exams you had to take was usually three or four and never more than five. You were only tested on one subject at a time, you knew which subject it was going to be, and then you had at least one day (usually more) before you were tested on another subject. Typically, the material covered on the exam was limited to what the professor covered during the semester, whether in the assigned readings or in class discussions. Most professors probably gave you some idea of the topics to be tested and intimated what you should pay close attention to when studying. Some even gave a review class before the final. If you were lucky, your professor kept some old exams on file, and if you were really lucky, there were some sample answers on file too. This acted as a limit on the scope and nature of the material for which you were responsible. The result was that you had a pretty good idea of what to expect when you walked into the test.

In contrast, when you walk into the bar exam, you're facing what seems like the entire legal universe. You're responsible for all the subjects tested in your jurisdiction. Further, they are tested in a completely random manner so that both the subject matter and the level of difficulty may vary as you proceed from question to question. And to make matters that much worse, you're tested on everything in a two day period.

1. Finding the Bar Exam's Boundaries

Let's face it: you're never going to feel good about the bar exam but wouldn't you feel a lot better if you could define its scope and put yourself on the same footing as you did for law school exams? The good news is that you can because the bar exam has boundaries. You just need to know how to find them.

Bar review courses pretty much lead you to believe that you must read everything, learn everything, and do everything they tell you in the way that they tell you or you'll fail. The result is that you can end up feeling overwhelmed. This is neither productive nor necessary. Instead, you should trust the bar review course to give you all the law you need to know but look to the bar examiners and your own strengths and weaknesses to tailor a study program that puts you in control and not the other way around.

Make no mistake: you need to master the substantive law presented to you in the bar review course. However, the way you go about it is up to you. If you think about it, bar review courses are designed for the multitudes. These courses put together a master template of the law tested on the bar exam. And they do a real good job of it. They structure and sequence the topics, adapt the material for your particular jurisdiction, and factor in some application as well. They provide an organized approach to study and that's what you need. But the "one size fits all" approach is not necessarily the way to go—not in your wardrobe and not in your studies.

But I can hear you now: "what do I know about making my own study plan? Shouldn't I just leave it to the experts?" Yes, you should, but not without considering all of the experts.

- Aren't the bar examiners "experts" on the bar exam?

- Aren't you an "expert" on how you study and how you learn?

- Aren't you the "expert" when it comes to knowing your strengths and weaknesses?

Shouldn't you at least consider the voices of these experts as well as the bar review experts? Just ask yourself the following questions:

- Who is creating the exam and who is grading it?
- Are all the topics accorded equal treatment on the exam?
- Are some topics tested more than others?
- How are the topics tested in essays?
- Am I more familiar and comfortable with some areas of the law than others?

2. It's Time to Meet the Bar Examiners

The National Conference of Bar Examiners ("NCBE") develops the multistate portions of the bar exam; the individual state boards of law examiners develop their own state-specific components. Together, they determine whether or not you'll practice law.

Each jurisdiction administers the exam and determines its own policy with regard to the relative weight given to the scores for each component of the bar exam. Typically, your bar review course will provide this information for you; it's also available to you from your jurisdiction and any inquiries about the relative weight given to such scores should therefore be directed to your state board of law examiners and not the NCBE.

If I were you, and I was not too long ago, I'd be interested in anything and everything the Bar Examiners have to say about the bar exam. It's all too easy to overlook this primary source of inside information in your haste to get to your "official" bar review materials. Nonetheless, the information prepared and released by the Bar Examiners should figure prominently in your collection of study materials.

The Bar Examiners give you the real scoop on the bar exam. This is true of both the national and state bar examiners. The NCBE provides specific subject matter outlines indicating the scope of coverage for each of the topics covered on the exam. For example, there is an outline for each of the six Multistate Bar Examination subjects: Constitutional Law, Contracts, Criminal Law, Property, Evidence, and Torts. These subject outlines are extremely useful. Not only is each potential test topic identified within each subject, you're also given a breakdown by percentage of how many questions will be taken from a particular category. It might be nice to know, therefore, that of the 33 real property/future interests question on the MBE, only 25% (8–9 questions) come from real property contracts and mortgages. So if mortgages happen to be your most dreaded topic, the likelihood that you'll see more than four or five actual mortgage questions is extremely unlikely. On the other hand, it is very important to know that of the 34 torts questions, approximately one-half of them will be negligence questions. With 17 questions, which represents almost 8.5% of the entire MBE, you can't afford to treat negligence issues lightly when you study.

As you study, these subject outlines will be an invaluable resource to you. You will use them to target and focus your energies. Doesn't it make sense to allocate your time and effort to those subjects where you have the greatest likelihood of increasing your score? How practical would it be to spend precious study days on a particularly difficult topic for you when it might be at most two or three questions on the exam? We'll be discussing such techniques in greater detail when we examine each section of the bar exam.

In addition to giving you valuable information on the Multistate Bar Examination, the NCBE also provides information on the Multistate Performance Test ("MPT") and the Multistate Essay Examination ("MEE"). These are two other components of the bar exam developed by the NCBE. However, while almost every state administers the MBE portion of the exam, the same is not true for the MPT and the MEE. As of July, 1997, only three states do not administer the MBE. These states are Louisiana, Indiana, and Washington. So unless you're from one of these states, or plan to move there to practice law, you're stuck with the MBE. As you can see, you must know the specific components administered in your jurisdiction. The NCBE recommends that applicants contact the jurisdiction where admission is being sought. A regularly updated list of each jurisdiction's bar admission office phone number and address can be found at *www.ncbex.org,* the NCBE's official website.

Also, the NCBE publishes individual Information Booklets on the MBE, MPT, and MEE. These booklets provide the bar applicant with a general description of the test, outlines of the subject matter covered, and sample questions. For example, the MBE Information Booklet contains the subject outlines we've already discussed. In addition, it contains sample questions and an order form to order previously published MBE questions. What does this mean? It means you have access to actual bar exam questions. These are questions the Bar Examiners have retired from use. What could be better to practice from than actual questions?

Unlike the MBE which has been a staple of the bar exam for well over 20 years, the MPT is a relative newcomer. Currently, twenty-seven states test lawyering skills by administering the MPT. In July of 2001, New York joined twenty-six other states in administering the MPT, the most substantive change to New York's bar exam in more than twenty years. There are other states that plan to add the MPT in the future and some, like California, have long since adopted their own version of the MPT. Apparently, the trend toward making the bar exam a test of a candidate's practical lawyering skills is gaining momentum and even if it is not currently part of your own state's licensing exam, chances are that it will be in the near future.

Once again, the NCBE is an invaluable ally in your studies. Just as it has published released Multistate questions, the NCBE has made available previously released MPTs. A number of them are available for downloading from the NCBE's website. Additional MPTs and Point Sheets (points sheets are the scoring guidelines suggested by the NCBE in preparing the question, but more about these in the MPT chapter) are available by ordering them from the MPT Study Aids Order Form at the end of the MPT Information Booklet. You will want the opportunity to practice from as many as possible to sample the various task possibilities you might encounter on the MPT.

The MEE is also developed by the NCBE and administered by participating jurisdictions on the state day of the exam. The MEE is the essay portion of the exam and as the Information Booklet informs us, the areas of law that may be covered include: Agency and Partnership, Commercial Paper, Conflict of Laws, Corporations, Decedents' Estates, Family Law, Federal Civil Procedure, Sales, Secured Transactions, and Trusts and Future Interests. Some questions may contain issues from more than one area of law.

Here, too, the NCBE provides candidates with the opportunity to work from previously released MEE questions. Several examples are included in the Information Booklet and more are available for purchase. If your jurisdiction uses the MEE, then I strongly suggest that you order the additional MEE questions. Not only does each test includes seven questions, but it includes model analyses for each of the questions. According to the NCBE in its Preface to an MEE booklet, these models are "illustrative of the discussions that might appear in excellent answers to the questions. They are provided to the user jurisdictions for the sole purpose of assisting graders in grading the examination." Wouldn't you want to know what the graders will be looking for in your essay? I would. We'll be discussing essays, both the MEE and individual state essays, in great detail in the essay writing chapter.

Like the NCBE, the individual state bar examiners make vital information available to its bar candidates. It's all right there for you on the internet. In fact, the first website you need to add to your list of favorites is the bar examiner's site in your particular jurisdiction. Your state board of bar examiners is really your point of contact for most, if not all, of your bar-related questions.

Each jurisdiction administers the exam and determines its own policy with regard to the relative weight given to the scores for each component of the bar exam. As a result, you'll want to be very familiar with the requirements and standards of your particular jurisdiction. It is your primary source for such basic information as application materials, test locations and accommodations, test dates, admissions issues, and more. Even more importantly, most jurisdictions include some examples of past exam questions and sample answers. These samples will figure prominently in your study plan. While you'll have a good number of simulated practice tests and essay writing exercises in your bar review course, there is no substitute for the original and here there is no need for substitutes because the real thing is readily available.

C. SOME COMMON SENSE STUDY STRATEGIES

For the most part, you should leave the substantive portion of your study plan to your bar review course. As I've said before, they specialize in putting together the right mix of black letter law that you'll need to know for the bar exam in your jurisdiction. Your job, on the other hand, is to determine how best to supplement or adapt what they provide to serve your needs.

1. All Subjects Are Not Created Equal

First, realize that you do not need to study all subjects with equal intensity. For the MBE, you can use the subject outlines for the MBE as your guide and identify which sub-topics within each particular subject tend to be more difficult for you. These are the areas where you'll need to devote more of your study time. For example, if your course devotes but one lecture to contract remedies and you find that this is your weak spot, then you'll need to spend more time on it than the review course study schedule allocates. This is just being sensible. But sometimes when you're caught up in the hysteria of the bar review period, it's easy to forget that as the one principally in charge of your study program, you may need to change it to suit your needs.

Also, remember that the MBE does not treat all topics equally in terms of their significance on the exam; consequently, you don't have to devote equal study time to all topics. While it is absolutely essential to learn the substantive law thoroughly, you can use your judgment in allocating your time and efforts to where it will do you the most good. For example, since some MBE subjects are easier to master, and if time is a factor, you should consider focusing your energy on questions in those areas you're likely to find easier to answer. Based on my work with students and my own assessment of the questions, the most difficult MBE questions tend to be property, contracts, and evidence. Property and contracts questions are the longest to read and contain the most specific, detailed, factual information. The questions tend to contain several transactions and several parties which means that they take longer to read and thus there is a greater likelihood of misreading or overlooking some key fact. On the other hand, while evidence questions tend to be short hypotheticals, they usually require several levels of analysis to reach an answer. This too takes time and provides a greater opportunity for error.

2.   Know your Weakness: Is it Essays or Multiple Choice?

Second, identify which particular type of question poses more of a difficulty for you. Consider your academic career: have you typically scored lower on objective tests than essay tests? Are you like me and when it comes to choosing between two answers, it seems I always make the wrong choice? If so, then you're going to want to devote more of your study time to learning how to analyze objective questions.

Alternatively, if your professors consistently found much to be lacking in your essays, then you're going to consider spending more time on developing your essay writing skills. I'm not suggesting that this is the time to learn to write for law review, but you can learn to write quality essays that rack up the points on the bar exam. In fact, most of my work with repeat candidates has been in this area and the results have been impressive. As we'll be discussing shortly, the essay portion of the bar exam is where you have the greatest opportunity to influence the outcome. Consequently, it's the part of the exam where this book can be of the most value to you.

3. Set Realistic Study Goals

For many students, getting started in their study program follows one of two possible directions, each one based in large part on the student's own personality. The first is the "gung-ho" approach. Here the student plunges wildly into the fray, vowing to study 14 hours a day, complete every bar review assignment, read every outline, and do at least 100 multiple choice questions a day. While there is much to be said for enthusiasm, this poor snook won't survive a week at this frantic pace. Not only is this kind of schedule impossible to maintain, it's guaranteed to lead to burn-out.

The second approach is what I call the "Scarlett O'Hara" philosophy. In this case, the student can't bear to think about the reality of the bar exam and believes that there's always tomorrow to get serious about studying. So what if a bar review class or two is missed. What's the big deal? There's always the tape backup for missed sessions. The problem with this mind-set is that there's no time to waste. You can no more "ease into" bar review than you could "ease into" law school. Each day counts; there's no making up for lost time.

My advice is to strike a balance between the overly aggressive approach and the overly complacent approach. You can do this by setting realistic goals for yourself. If you know that there's no way you're going to get through 50 or 100 multiple choice questions a day, don't set such an unreasonable goal. Why set yourself up for failure? You must be able to sustain the effort over the entire review period, up to and including the bar exam itself. It's no good if you burn out too soon. Besides, as we'll discuss in the next chapter, the objective in practicing multiple choice questions is not the "doing" of numbers but the learning of law and analysis.

4. Avoid Burnout and Boredom

You can avoid early burn out by maintaining a realistic work schedule, one that allows for lecture time, review time, practice time, and relaxation time. For the most part, your day will be centered around your bar review course. Typically, these courses are offered both during the day and the evening. You should choose your section carefully. While some of you may have no choice but to go in the evening because of work or family obligations, others may consider the evening section desirable because of a general failure to function before noon. If this is you, think again. You'll need to be wide awake and focused at 9:00 a.m. on exam day. I strongly recommend that you consider taking a morning review session to acclimate yourself to concentrating at this hour. It takes time to condition yourself to become a morning person and this is the perfect (and probably the only) opportunity to do it in time for the bar exam.

Once you've made your choice, stick with it. Don't alternate class sections unless you need to make up a missed class. You want to get used to a regular work schedule. While it may seem strange to you now, you'll find comfort in a familiar routine. Even if you fought the predictability of a routine existence all your life, give up the battle for the next two months and let your body and mind have what it needs to function at its best. Eat regularly, sleep regularly, exercise regularly, and study regularly. And don't forget to take breaks regularly.

As you can well imagine, one of the most serious challenges you'll face as you study for the bar exam will be to maintain your focus. After a couple of weeks spent in the relentless routine of going to bar review class, reviewing your notes, and practicing the questions, you'll see what I mean. It's easy to lose momentum and become stuck in a study rut. An effective way to avoid this trap is to divide your study time between tasks. This helps to avoid the boredom.

In addition to varying your activities throughout the day, you'll want to study from different materials. The truth is that not only do your notes lose their appeal after the second read (and some would claim well before this), they also lose their ability to engage your mind simply because you're familiar with what's there. It's like listening to a song on the radio. The first time you hear the song, you pay attention and listen carefully. The next time you hear it come on the radio, you're interested but pay less attention because you've heard it before. Your mind drifts and you think of other things. Well, the same phenomenon occurs when you study. You think you're studying but you've really stopped paying attention because it's already familiar to you. You're putting in the time, but you've stopped deriving any true benefit from it. In this case, what you need to do is alternate your review materials. Take up the particular topic in another form—read a different outline from your bar review materials, go back to your own outline from law school, or consider a hornbook—anything that keeps you interested and adds to your understanding of the subject.

5.   A Day in the Life

While one schedule won't suit all, I still think it's valuable to give you an example of a typical day. I'll describe what mine was like—not because you must necessarily adapt it as your own, but because it's an example of one that worked.

I opted for an evening review course because I had been an evening student in law school and had gotten used to being productive in the evening. Also, I think it relevant to tell you that I graduated in December and sat for a February bar exam. This meant that I was studying during the winter months, when the days are short and you don't mind being indoors. After the excitement of the holidays, there are few if any distractions. The sounds of summer that tend to beckon and distract are absent and all you're left with are short, dark days well suited for study.

Still, if you're to graduate in May, you should sit for the July exam. Even if the February bar now seems to offer some advantages, these do not outweigh the benefit of coming to the exam straight from the rigors of your law school education. Unless you have some extraordinary reasons for doing so, don't postpone the bar exam. Even a few months away from your studies can have a significant impact. It's much harder to get back into the routine when you've been away from it for a while. And if you think that you'll devote all the extra time you have to studying, trust me—you won't. You won't start studying in May when you know you're not taking the exam until February. My experience with students, and just plain common sense, shows that this doesn't happen.

The following was an average day for me:

AM
7:30—8:30   Eat breakfast, read newspaper, shower, and dress

Note: This would vary. Three or four times a week I added a 30–minute exercise period to my routine. Exercise is very important during this time of intense concentration. If you already exercise, keep it up. If you don't, then start. All you have to do is take a brisk walk. Even if it's only 30 minutes every other day or so, it will make a significant difference in how you feel and how you work.

8:30—10:30   Review notes from the previous evening's class.
Make index cards for rules of law.

Note: It would take about two hours to read and review the approximately 20 pages of notes taken from the previous evening's four hour class.

10:30—11:00   Coffee break; take pup for a walk

11:00—1:00   Practice multiple choice questions in the area of law I had been reviewing.

Note: I would answer a question or the group of questions based on a fact pattern and then check my answers. Even if I answered correctly, I would read the explanations. If I got the answer wrong,

I would go back to the question and go through it again to determine where I had erred: was it in the reading of the question? Did I not know the rule? I didn't move on to another question until I was satisfied that I understood what was going on in that question and why I had gotten it wrong. If necessary, I would return to my outline or consult a hornbook on the topic in question. This meant that sometimes I covered only 15 or so questions in a two hour period. But after this time, I felt comfortable that I had really truly something.

1:00—1:30   Lunch. Phone calls. Laundry.

1:30—3:00   More multiple choice practice.

Note: As the weeks went by, I would vary my work during this time to include essay reading and writing. Depending on the requirements of your jurisdiction, I would alternate this period to accommodate the different parts of the exam.

3:00—4:00   Watch *General Hospital*. Fold the laundry.

Note: Some things are sacred. You don't have to give up everything.

4:00—5:00	Review syllabus to identify what would be covered next in bar review class. Review index cards to work on memorizing elements of rules of law/ review subject studied earlier in the course.
Note:	I would focus on one subject at a time and alternate between subjects to make sure that I kept reviewing the material that I had learned earlier.
	Give pup dinner and take her for a walk.
	Have a snack.
5:15	Leave for bar review class
6:00—10:00	Bar review class
Note:	Evening review classes are difficult because they pretty much eliminate any regular dinner hour. But you can't afford not to eat or to eat improperly. Sometimes I would have a snack before class or I would pack a sandwich and eat during class. Figure out which works best for you and make sure you have some healthy snack foods available.
10:30	Home. Talk to husband.

11:00   Relax. Watch *Law and Order*.
                         Pass out.

In looking at how I spent my days, I see that I didn't do much of anything but study. If you ask whether I ever went to the supermarket or cleaners or post office, the answer is "no." But then again, I never went to these places: my husband always took care of such matters. For my part, I continued to do some general household stuff, but the day went by so quickly that there just wasn't time for anything else.

I found studying for the bar to be all consuming. I would become so immersed in my studies that I found it difficult to switch gears and didn't feel like doing anything else. Don't be surprised if you find yourself feeling this way too. It's the natural result of focusing so intently and, for the most part, it's what you need to be doing—and what you should be doing during this time.

However, this is not to say that my routine never varied. Of course it did. Also, during the first half of the bar review period, I would take an afternoon or evening off at least once a week. I would do something enjoyable or just get out of the house: I would go shopping, visit my parents, take care of errands, and go out to dinner with my husband. I would try to relax but I know I wasn't great company because I was always preoccupied. If I wanted to take a break, I found it best to simply watch TV or go to a movie. In fact, movies were the best diversion because it was the only time I would be able to stop thinking about the law I had been studying. I highly recommend regular movie breaks.

It's important during these weeks to keep a positive attitude. When it gets difficult and you feel overwhelmed, take a break. If you find yourself reading the same paragraph over and over again, and still don't know what you've just read, stop immediately and do something different. Either change what you're working on or get up and go for a walk. It's not productive to keep at it when you're not deriving any benefit from the effort. It just makes you tired and adds to your stress. A short break works wonders. You need to relieve the tension and gain your perspective. It helps to realize that you're not alone and that thousands of students take their state's bar exams every year and pass. They're not any smarter than you.

CHAPTER 4

DE–CONSTRUCTING
THE BAR EXAM

A. INTRODUCING "FORENSIC IRAC"

As I explained earlier, the key to answering bar
exam questions successfully is to engage in IRAC
analysis. Sadly, too many bar candidates neglect to
do so—much to their subsequent lament. In these
cases, it isn't so much that IRAC analysis is absent
entirely, but that its use is flawed or inadequate.
The real problem is that these students can't tell
the difference between the two: they tend to be so
disconnected from their own thought process that
they continue to make the same mistakes over and
over again, blaming everything from poor study
habits to nervousness instead of acknowledging
what's right in front of them.

Fortunately, however, IRAC is a process and I've
identified several techniques for tracking that process. I've termed it "forensic IRAC" because these
techniques are similar to those employed by crime
scene investigators, accountants, medical examiners, and any of the "so-called" forensic experts who
go back over the trail of evidence to determine
precisely how that evidence led to a particular result. While such experts rely on fingerprints, ledger

books, and DNA to find their culprit, we use IRAC . We work backward from the incorrect exam answer using IRAC analysis to figure out how and what you were thinking that led you to select that answer choice or write that essay response. It's somewhat ironic that we use IRAC analysis to find the flaw in our IRAC application, but it makes sense given the process of legal thought and the dynamics of the exam.

While all the questions on the bar exam require an IRAC analysis, different parts of the exam emphasize different elements of the IRAC equation. Consequently, our techniques will vary according to the skills tested by the particular type of question. As we discuss each component of the bar exam, an important part of the de-constructing process will be engaging in the forensic technique appropriate to that component. Accordingly, we'll demonstrate and practice each technique in the context of the exam, beginning with essay writing, but for now a brief illustration will help you understand the process.

B. HOW IT WORKS

Answering a multiple choice question relies most heavily on reading skills to identify the issue or the legal question presented by the facts in the hypothetical. Of course you must know rules of law to find the legal question and then arrive at the correct answer choice, but if you miss the signals in the question by failing to identify significant language, confuse the parties by mixing up who is doing what to whom, skip over key passages, or simply misread the language, you won't be able to frame the issue correctly. Therefore, if you made an error in a multiple choice question, I would ask you to go back to that question, reread it, and ask yourself the following questions before you select another answer choice:

- What area of law is implicated?
- What do I think is happening in this problem?
- Based on what's happening, what facts in the question do I think are legally significant?
- What do I think is the legal problem presented by the facts?
- What do I think should be the outcome or answer to this question?

While these are very basic questions, they nonetheless force you to engage in active reading by making you question what you read. This keeps you focused on what's going on in the fact pattern and prevents you from straying into irrelevant territory and making unsubstantiated assumptions and inferences. And most importantly, it ensures that you examine the answer choices with a response already in mind. Instead of viewing choices (A)–(D) as a universe of possibilities, you've already narrowed the field to what you've determined should be the answer. Now you just need to find the words that "match up" with what you have in mind.

The difference in approaching questions like this is like the difference between going to a restaurant with no idea of what you'd like to order and finding everything on the menu appealing as compared to going to the restaurant knowing you want a steak and potatoes dinner. Immediately you've eliminated all the chicken, fish, and pasta and what's left is the steak.

C. APPLYING THE TECHNIQUE

Now you're in a position to answer the question. Invariably, you'll answer differently than you did the first time. But after you've made your answer choice, your work is not done. You need to understand what you were thinking the first time around. *So, in an effort to recreate your thought process the first time, you're going to go back through these same questions, retrace your steps, and compare your answers in the two instances to find where you diverged in your analysis.* In this simple but highly instructive manner, you can determine whether the problem was in a reading or misreading of the facts, a failure to recognize legally significant language, an ignorance of the rule, or a misapplication of law to facts.

In working with students, I've found this process to be highly informative. It lets us narrow the field of possibilities and focus our energies on where they can be most productive. For example, if we find that you tend to answer questions incorrectly because you confuse the parties or mix up the sequence of events, then we can work on your reading skills. Typically, this means slowing you down because you tend to read carelessly when you read too quickly. Similarly, if we find that you select answer choices that have no foundation in the facts, we usually find that you're the type who is subject to "straying." This means that your mind wanders and you read facts into the problem that are not there. Once again, by getting you to read actively, we eliminate this issue.

Let's see how this process works by revisiting our friends Peavey and Dorwin for a moment. Suppose we answered this question incorrectly the first time, selecting the popular but incorrect Answer Choice D. If we ask the first question, "what area of the law are we in?" we should conclude that it's a torts case. That's important because you want to apply the right rule of law. Students who failed to consider what area of law they were in proceeded from the flawed premise that it was a criminal battery case. How do I know this is what they were thinking? I know because I asked them to tell me what led them to think that Dorwin's best defense was that Peavey was about to attack him. Invariably, they answered that it was because self defense is a valid justification for a criminal attack. As we saw earlier, this reasoning is flawed for several reasons but in this context, we're concerned with two specific reading errors: first, is the error of the "straying" variety. Here the facts tell us that Peavey brought the action against Dorwin. This makes it a civil case, not a criminal case. If Dorwin was a criminal actor, then the state would have brought the action. Having strayed from the facts and assumed that it was a criminal action, then self-defense became a plausible answer. Unfortunately, this type of creative reading simply puts the student on the path to the wrong answer choice.

The second type of error is of the "careless reading" variety. In this instance, the facts tell us Peavey was walking "peacefully" and it was "without provocation or warning, [that] Dorwin picked up a rock." Clearly, the reader failed to note the significance of this language or skipped over it entirely, in either case leading to the selection of an incorrect answer choice. The general result of these types of reading comprehension problems is a failure to identify the issue raised by the facts. Our forensic analysis, therefore, led us to the "issue" in IRAC as the source of our problem.

In contrast, a problem with the "rule" in IRAC manifests itself differently. In this case the student correctly identifies the issue but subsequently misapplies the rule to the facts or simply fails to recognize the rule from the language presented in the answer choice. Returning to our Peavey problem, if the student had selected either Answer Choice A or B, then the error would have been a failure to understand and apply the "intent" element correctly. Here the student would have considered the definition of a battery as the intentional infliction of a harmful or offensive bodily contact but failed to acknowledge the other possibility: whether the tortfeasor did the act *knowing with substantial certainty* that a harmful or offensive contact would result.

Hence, forensic IRAC has led us to see a weakness in our understanding of the "rule." Typically, when forensic analysis shows a problem in this area, it's either because of an overly simplistic understanding of the rule or a basic lack of knowledge. As you'll see, you need to know the rules with specificity in order to distinguish between the answer choices. The solution to this kind of problem is more study time devoted to learning the rules and their elements in the context in which they are tested.

I know that this must sound like an awful lot to do when you have only 1.8 minutes for each Multistate question. Fortunately, however, the thought process becomes so mechanical through practice that it's automatic by test day. You'll find that you can manage effectively within the given time constraints.

Now it's time to move on to the individual components of the bar exam and learn specific strategies and techniques.

CHAPTER 5

BAR EXAM ESSAYS

A. WRITING IS A DIALOGUE

Before we discuss specific strategies for writing successful bar exam essays, let's talk about writing in general: I'm sure a good number of you have been very successful in law school and a large part of that success can be credited to your ability to communicate effectively in writing. For you, doing well on the essay portion of the bar exam will be a simple matter of gaining familiarity with the types of essays on the bar and their structure. But for those of you for whom essays posed a bit more of a challenge, I want you to know that you too can do well on bar exam essays. There is a method to scoring points and this is what I am going to share with you.

If you think about it, you'll realize that the essays are your **opportunity to converse** with the bar examiners. With every word you write, your goal is to tell the grader that you are prepared to take your place in the profession—that you are ready to meet with clients, analyze their problems, and represent them in court.

How do you convey this message? By using the **language of the law** in the format and structure

56

of legal analysis. This is the only way to demonstrate your competency to join the bar. Presumably, after reading hundreds of cases, you sound something like a lawyer. When a grader reads your essay, there should be "a scintilla of evidence" to show that you've attended law school.

This is a very important concept and deserves your closest attention. Using the appropriate terminology in your discussion of a legal issue is what sets you apart from a layperson. The presumption is that only one who has gone to law school and studied the law would speak in terms of the *mens rea* required to satisfy the elements of the crime or whether impossibility is a valid defense to a charge of attempt. Shouldn't there be a demonstrable difference between a graduate of a legal education and an avid fan of courtroom television?

B. HERE'S YOUR CHANCE TO INFLU-ENCE THE OUTCOME

The essay portion of the bar exam presents the greatest opportunity for you to influence your score because when you write, you're the one in control. You're in the driver's seat, taking the grader through the steps of your legal analysis and demonstrating your competence. Unlike a multiple choice question where you have to match up your analysis of the problem precisely into one of the set answer choices, here you have some flexibility. While there are parameters determined by the issues set up in the facts, you can take a slightly different path and still accrue significant points. Depending on your jurisdiction, the weight given to your essay score can be as much as 55% of your entire grade, as it is in New Jersey. It would be just plain foolishness not to make the most of such an opportunity.

C. WRITING SUCCESSFUL ESSAY AN-SWERS: WHAT IT TAKES ACCORDING TO THE BAR EXAMINERS

1. Analysis, Not Answers

The bar examiners are very clear about what they want from you. Whether in directions to applicants in state publications, posted on web sites, or in the bulletins of the National Conference of Bar Examiners, the bar examiners tell you exactly what they expect and they all expect the same thing: an essay that demonstrates your ability to engage in legal thought and analysis. The bar examiners are not looking for a "right answer" or a bottom line answer—if you thought this was the case, you should have gone to business school. Your "conclusion" is largely irrelevant: it serves only to provide a logical close to your argument. And that's precisely what the bar examiners are looking for when grading your essay: a well-reasoned argument based on an analysis of the relevant issues and an application of the law to the facts followed by a legal conclusion.

The ability to reason in a logical, lawyer-like manner is so important that you can get credit for your analysis even if you technically arrive at the incorrect conclusion. The New York Board of Law

Examiners advise that "[a]ppropriate credit is given in the grading of essay answers for well reasoned analyses of the issues and legal principles involved even though the final conclusion may be incorrect."

The National Conference of Bar Examiners similarly instructs its candidates that "the value of your answer depends not as much upon your conclusions as upon the presence and quality of the elements mentioned above." These elements include an understanding of the facts, a recognition of the issues, the applicable principles of law, and the reasoning by which the conclusion is reached.

Consequently, as you review sample candidate answers, you will find examples of answers that reach opposite conclusions yet have been selected as above average answers. You should pay particular attention to such examples because it's tangible proof of what we've been saying all along—that it's the reasoning that counts and not the bottom line conclusion.

2. Identification of the Legal Issue

In addition to the admonition to write an orderly and logical analysis in a lawyer-like manner, no single direction is repeated more often by bar examiners than the need to identify the legal issue. The candidate's ability to identify the legal issue raised by a set of facts is so essential that the National Conference of Bar Examiners identify it as the first skill it seeks to test with the Multistate Essay Examination. In its Information Booklet on the MEE, the bar examiners identify the purpose of the essays as a test of the candidate's abilities in four critical areas, listing the ability "to identify legal issues raised by a hypothetical factual situation" as first, followed in order by the need "to separate material which is relevant from that which is not; [to] present a reasoned analysis of the relevant issues in a clear, concise, and well organized composition; and [to] demonstrate an understanding of the fundamental legal principles relevant to the probable solution of the issues raised by the factual situation."

The New York Board of Law Examiners provides its candidates with these guidelines:

Each essay question is designed to test the applicant's ability to analyze a given set of facts, to identify the issues involved and the applicable principles of law, and to reason therefrom to a sound conclusion. An essay answer should show a recognition of each issue presented by the material facts, discuss the principles of law applicable thereto and set forth the reasoning by which the conclusion has been reached. The answer should be clear and concise. It should be confined to the particular issues presented and should not include information that is not responsive to the question.

Similarly, the New Jersey Board of Bar Examiners provides directions to its candidates on answering essay questions, again focusing on the ability "to identify and analyze issues and to present an organized, coherent and well-written response within the prescribed format." So critical is the ability to write clearly that the New Jersey Board members found it important enough to include a list of five general writing and organizational tips, reminding candidates of such basics as the need to outline before writing, structuring an answer to avoid a "scattershot" approach, and allocating enough time to compose a "clear and concise response."

As you can see, the information provided by the bar examiners will be critical to your success on the bar exam for two very important reasons: first, it forces you to recognize the need to IRAC your answers, and second, it gives you all the elements for a model answer. For all practical purposes, you need look no further than the exam descriptions from your particular jurisdiction for a guide to writing successful essays. If this is what your bar examiner tells you to do, why would you do anything else? Common sense alone should tell you to do what you're told.

Sometimes, however, even common sense needs a helping hand. Therefore, in the examples that follow, you'll learn how to use these suggestions to demonstrate your knowledge and make it easy for the grader to give you points.

D. OUTLINING THE STRATEGY

The single most important strategy for passing the bar exam is not a strategy at all but a matter of common sense: you must know the law to write the law. Unfortunately, too many candidates walk into the bar exam without knowing enough black letter law. There is no substitute for knowledge of the law: you must know the rules with specificity both to identify the legal problem presented by the facts and to write a comprehensive answer that gets points.

1. Know the Rules

Memorization is essential to your mastery of the law. As you proceed through your bar review course, make it a priority to memorize basic definitions and the elements of rules for each subject. At first this will seem artificial, even mechanical. But remember when you were in grade school and had to learn the multiplication tables? You used flash cards and repeated the tables over and over again until you knew them cold. The same principle applies here. Make index cards for the definitions and rules and study them until you know them verbatim. Focus on the basic vocabulary of each subject. While you may begin by rote memorization, you end up knowing the material and this knowledge becomes part of you—for the exam and in practice.

To ensure that you understand as well as memorize the rules, practice each rule in terms of a hypothetical. Play around with the facts of the hypothetical. Ask yourself whether the change affects the outcome. For example, if you are studying criminal law, ask yourself whether it's a burglary when the entering of the apartment occurred at 4:30 pm? At 8:30 pm? Apply different rules to the same scenario. What if you apply the common law to this set of facts? What if you apply the rule in your jurisdiction? Same result or different result? This type of practice provides the context you need for understanding as well as memorizing the rules of law.

2.   Write IRAC

While the substantive law differs between the jurisdictions, the technique required to write effective essays remains the same: the diligent application of IRAC analysis. With but a slight modification or two, IRAC forms the basic structure of your essay. It's your formula for success because it's the essence of legal analysis and allows you to organize your responses in a way that makes sense. It's also where the points are to be found.

In some jurisdictions, the bar examiners will ask you to come to a conclusion with respect to the question they've asked you to consider. What's important when you're asked to provide a conclusion is that you take a position and argue it. Unlike a typical law school exam, here you are not supposed to argue in the alternative and present both points of view. In conclusion-based jurisdictions, you're suppose to be an advocate and demonstrate how you marshal the facts to the law.

Soon we'll examine each of the IRAC elements individually in terms of how to write them but for now a brief overview will introduce you to the essential elements.

3. The Individual IRAC Elements

a. *The Issue*

The issue is the most important element in the analysis because you need to know enough law to find the issue. You should strive to articulate the issue by formulating the legal question presented by the facts. Ask yourself: *"what is the theory"* or *"what is in controversy"* in these facts. That is the issue. Even in those jurisdictions that favor such general open-ended interrogatories as "analyze fully," you should strive to identify the issue and sub-issues as completely as possible in terms of the rule and which facts bring that rule into controversy. Not only does this earn points from the grader, but it ensures that you will be on the right path in your analysis. Furthermore, once you get the grader to like your paper by starting out on the right foot with a nice statement of the issue, it's pretty hard not to get a good score.

b. *The Rule*

The issue leads you to the statement of the rule needed to resolve the issue. State it completely. The major problem for most candidates is deciding what to include and they end up by writing either too much or too little. The general "rule" to follow when writing the "rule" is to include a sufficient discussion of the law to provide an adequate context for your analysis of the facts in controversy.

c. *Application, not Recitation*

Examine the inferences/implications of each fact in light of the rule. Look for the ambiguities in interpreting the facts. Focus on explaining how these facts can be interpreted. Application is analysis. It is explaining to the reader the legal significance and consequence of that fact. Generally, candidates miss a golden opportunity to accrue much needed points in this area. After all, once you've identified the rule, all you have to do is discuss the facts with respect to each of the identified elements. However, your job is not to merely repeat the facts. There are no points given for recitation, only application.

d. *Conclusion*

State your general conclusion. Once again, there is no right or wrong answer. There is only logical analysis based on the rule and the facts which lead to a reasonable conclusion.

4.   Practice from the Source

There is no substitute for the real thing. There is no better way to prepare for the bar exam than to work from past bar exams. Working with actual questions provides familiarity with the structure, substance, and style of your exam and gives you a true sense of what to expect on bar day. As we discussed earlier, a good number of jurisdictions have made their past exam questions available to you—some provide sample answers, either student essays or suggested analyses. By reviewing and analyzing released exams and sample answers from your jurisdiction, you can target your energies and gain a universe of experience in seeing how the topics come together and what is expected of you in response.

5. The General Types of State Bar Essay Questions

As you review the released questions, you'll find that they conform to one of two general essay styles. For illustration purposes, I'll refer to the first type as the "New York model" and the second type as the "New Jersey model."

a. The New York Model

In New York and many other jurisdictions including the MEE, the essay question is narrow and issue based: it asks you to come to a conclusion by answering a particular question. *Was the court correct in granting the motion for summary judgment/ for the injunction/ to admit the testimony? Can the defendant successfully assert the defense of justification?*

This type of question can prove troublesome for two reasons: first, it is unlike most law school exams in that it asks you to come to a single conclusion. While the conclusion you reach is relatively unimportant, your ability to marshal the law and the facts and argue for only one appropriate outcome is highly critical. It demonstrates your ability to reason through a series of legal principles to arrive at a logical conclusion based on an application of the facts to the law.

Second, this type of problem is challenging because the precise issue is not as clear as the interrogatory would at first lead you to believe. The question is not "whether the court was correct or incorrect" but whether the legal theory the court relied upon in coming to that decision was correct or incorrect. And of course this "legal theory" is not given to you but merely implied by the facts. Identifying the particular legal theory in controversy requires a multi-step analysis of the facts. Still, the extra minute or two it takes to think through the problem and articulate the precise issue in dispute is well worth the effort: it leads to an essay that is focused and connects the rules to the question asked instead of one that rambles and follows a "kitchen sink" approach.

And finally, this type of question requires that you *not* raise opposing arguments. While typical law school exams are structured for you to see and argue both sides of an issue, this is not the case with this model of bar exam. You are required to come to a conclusion and argue specifically for that conclusion. Any time you spend identifying potential counter-arguments is a waste of your time and a loss of potential points.

b. *The New Jersey Model*

In contrast, the New Jersey type essay question is more general and open-ended. It is typical of your law school exams where you are asked to evaluate possible courses of conduct or competing theories of the case. Consequently, you'll see such familiar interrogatories as: "discuss the rights and liabilities of all parties," "discuss all possible causes of action," or "analyze fully." Such general questions test not only your knowledge of substantive law but your organizational skills as well. Moreover, in these types of questions, you may be asked to assume a role and write your answer in the form of a legal memorandum, an argument, an attorney or client letter, or a contract provision. Such formats are just devices for the examiners to use to determine whether you can adopt the appropriate tone, language, and format in your response. The challenge, therefore, lies in your ability to cover the relevant possibilities with the requisite level of detail without going astray. Once again, organizing your answer around the issue and sub-issues is the key to a focused, concise answer.

Now that we've identified what's needed for a well-composed essay and the general types of essays, let's see exactly how it's done.

E. IMPLEMENTING THE STRATEGY

What follows now is a step-by-step approach for taking the exam. It's a blueprint you can follow to guide you through your practice sessions and then implement on bar day. Following this plan saves time and prevents anxiety: if you know exactly what you're going to do, and practice the routine sufficiently, it becomes second nature to you by test day.

1. Allocating Your Time during Practice and on Bar Day

Learning to budget your time and working within that time is the only way to ensure that you'll complete the exam—or come as close as possible to answering every question. And your goal is to answer as many questions as possible, as completely as possible. Consequently, you begin working toward this goal the minute you start studying for the bar exam. Every practice essay you write is a dress rehearsal. This means that you practice writing your essays within what will be the time parameters in your jurisdiction.

Assume you're planning to take the New York State bar exam. In this case, you'll have between 40 and 45 minutes to write each essay. How do I know you have 45 minutes? Because I checked the New York State Board of Law Examiners' web site and learned the composition of the state portion of the exam. You'll get this kind of information from your bar review course or your own state's web site.

For your first couple of practice essays, you won't pay any attention to the clock. You just want to see how long it takes you to complete an essay. This is your *baseline* writing time. Don't be surprised or disheartened if it takes a lot longer than 45 minutes. This is normal the first time you approach new material and writing a bar-style essay is a new experience. Once you've established your writing baseline, you can concentrate on improving your time through practice.

Now let's suppose it's bar day where the first day of your bar exam is the state portion of the exam. Generally, this means that you'll be writing essays and taking the MPT, if it's given in your jurisdiction. Some jurisdictions, including New York, also include multiple choice questions based on state law. The actual components don't matter; what matters is that you know what to expect before you walk into the exam. Knowing the precise breakdown of the exam in terms of the number of essays and multiple choice questions allows you to figure out precisely how much time you have to answer each question. This in turn allows you to create a "timetable" for the exam. For example, in New York, you'll have three essays and 50 multiple choice questions in the morning's three hour and 15 minute session, hence the recommended 40 minutes per essay and 1.5 minutes per multiple choice question. In the three-hour afternoon session, you'll face two essays and the MPT where you'll allocate 45 minutes for each essay and 90 minutes for the MPT question.

The very first thing you'll do when you get your scrap paper and told you may begin is to write down your timetable. The following schedule is based on New York's morning session and should look something like this, assuming the exam begins at 9:00 a.m.:

9:00–9:40	Essay one
9:40–10:20	Essay two

| 10:20–11:00 | Essay three |
| 11:00–12:15 | Multiple choice questions |

If you prefer, you can begin with the multiple choice questions and then proceed to the essays. The sequence doesn't matter in the slightest; what does matter, however, is that you have a defined timetable and that you keep to it throughout the exam.

With some modifications, you'll do the same for the afternoon session and again for the Multistate portion of the exam. This schedule completely eliminates your need to think about the clock during the test. All you'll do is look at the piece of paper and the time. You'll know exactly where you're supposed to be throughout the exam.

The key, however, is to follow the schedule, even if you've not completed the current task. The bar examiners have calculated the time very carefully; to finish the exam, you must stay within the schedule. If you "borrow" time from one question for another, you run the risk of not getting to the other questions. Instead, when you reach "time" on a particular question and you're not finished, you'll complete the sentence you're writing and make a note on your outline for that question as to where you had to stop. Hopefully, when you've finished the other questions on the exam, you'll have time to return to the incomplete question. At the very least, you can provide a summary from your outline of how you'd complete the analysis.

2. Reading the Question

Typically, bar exam essays are highly structured, focused, and specific. They are not like some of the long, issue-laden narratives you've seen on law school exams. This is a good thing for several reasons, one of which is that you have more than enough time to read the question two or even three times. Unfortunately, many of the mistakes candidates make are the result of reading the question incorrectly rather than a genuine lack of knowledge. Do you really want to lose points when you know the rules but simply misread the question?

a. *Start at the End of the Question*

Always read the interrogatory at the end of the question first. The interrogatory, or "call of the question," will let you know what task is required of you. This will inform your subsequent reading of the fact pattern and ensure that you read "actively" for the information you need.

The following are typical of some of the interrogatories you can expect to see:

- Was the court's ruling correct as to each defendant? (NY: Feb. 1998)

- Did the Surrogate correctly admit Hal's will to probate? (NY: Feb. 1998)

- Thoroughly analyze the constitutional issues that Big Mall Multiplex can raise in its action. (Ct. July 2000)

- You are the law clerk to the judge assigned to the civil trial. Prepare a memorandum on the admissibility of each proposed offer of evidence. (NJ: Feb. 2002)

- Did Able have an obligation to inform the limited partners of Historical Society's offer? Explain. (MEE: Feb. 2000)

As you can see, there is valuable information in the interrogatory. You can often tell the area of law, the issue in controversy, and the nature of your task.

b. Read the fact pattern "actively"

Once you've read the interrogatory, you can read the entire question and focus on the information relevant to your task. For example, if you're asked to evaluate court rulings, you'll go and find those rulings in the fact pattern and use them as a framework to inform your reading. Similarly, if you're asked to evaluate constitutional issues on behalf of a particular party, you'll read the facts with an eye toward framing arguments from that party's perspective.

"Active reading" means that you identify the following:

- *The area of law and the legal relationship between the parties.*

  Make it a priority to determine the area of law on which you are being tested. It is critical to your ability to evaluate the facts that you know the general subject area. Your determination of what questions to ask depends entirely on the area of law. For example, you would ask one series of questions if the parties were involved in a transactions involving a sale of goods and another, quite different series of questions, if the parties were performing a construction contract.

Similarly, while we don't care about much about the names of parties except to keep them straight in our answer, we care very much about the legal significance of parties' relationships. For example, you want to look for such significant relationships as husband/wife, attorney/client, buyer/seller, landlord/tenant, employer/employee, parent/child, and teacher/student, among others. Such relationships figure prominently in bar questions because they test your ability to note distinctions in how the law treats such relationships. Here, you may be dealing with fiduciary duties, different standards of care, and additional obligations.

- *Amounts of money, dates, locations, quantities, and ages.*

Be sure to circle dollar amounts, dates and times, quantities of items, jurisdictional information, and any ages if they appear in the fact pattern. Such facts are vital: for want of a date, whole essays are lost!

Imagine if you fail to make note of the time sequence of events in a sales transaction. Your analysis of the offer, acceptance, times for delivery, and even the warranty periods may be way off. Similarly, if you fail to note the ages of the parties, you may miss a statutory issue or a standard of liability. Typically, money and location information indicate jurisdictional thresholds—you certainly don't want to miss these signals. Make it a point to consistently identify this information when you read fact patterns and you won't miss the details that make the difference.

● *The words "oral" and "written."*

These words figure prominently in contract, property, and evidence questions. They signal potential issues with the Statute of Frauds, enforceability of promises, transactions with respect to land, and even admissibility of certain kinds of testimony.

Some final caveats about reading fact patterns: never add or assume information unless you are told to do so specifically by the call of the question; never make assumptions; and finally, make sure you are clear about *who is doing what to whom* before you begin your analysis. You don't want to confuse the actors. After all, the grader will not be able to intuit that you meant to conclude that "Dan is not guilty of manslaughter" when you actually wrote "Vic."

3. Organizing Your Thoughts Into An Outline

Only clear, organized thoughts can give rise to coherent, comprehensible answers. Accordingly, after you've read the question and before you write your answer, you must organize your ideas into an outline based on a consideration of the relevant issues. While you won't have time to write the type of detailed outline you may be used to preparing for a research paper, this doesn't mean you can afford to skip the process entirely. If you take the time to organize your thinking and draft an outline around the relevant issues, you'll have the beginnings of a winning essay.

An outline for a bar exam essay is little more than a list of the rules of law you've identified from the issues in the fact pattern. Not only are you under such time constraints during the exam that there is no time to write more than a rules-based outline, but there is no need to do so because the bar questions are usually so well constructed that they are organized around the rules. Further, your outline cannot contain conclusions because you simply won't know what your conclusions will be until you have worked through an application of the law to the relevant facts. And finally, there is no need to write facts into your outline because the facts are already there in the problem. Why would you want to rewrite them? Consequently, what you're left with is a list of the relevant rules you've discerned from the issues. Each issue becomes a focal point around which you will write your analysis.

The difficulty, of course, lies in identifying the legal issues. The issues will come from one of two possible sources, depending on the particular form of the essay. For example, in the New York model, you will use the interrogatories to guide your articulation of the issue while in the New Jersey model, you will need to ascertain the issues directly from the fact patterns.

Let's see how this works.

a.   Finding issues in the New York Model

The following is Question Two from the July 2001 New York Bar Examination:

At about 2:00 p.m. on Sunday, May 20, 2001, Paul, a Suffolk County police officer, was patrolling in a commercial area. He suddenly heard the shattering of window glass from a closed store, Ann's Antiques, and the ringing of the store's alarm. When Paul looked across the street, he saw a woman running out of the antique store, carrying a lamp. Paul immediately chased the woman, but before he reached her, she accidentally ran into Mark, an elderly pedestrian, who fell and severely injured his head on the sidewalk. The woman ran away, but the lamp she had been carrying was lying on the street with a tag on it which read, "Ann's Antiques, $150."

Shortly after Mark fell, an ambulance drove him to a local hospital. There, the doctor told Mark, who was conscious, that there was internal bleeding in his head, that his condition was serious, and that Mark would require prompt surgery. Before losing consciousness, Mark told Paul, who was questioning him at the hospital, that the woman who knocked him down was Denise, a waitress who worked at a nearby restaurant. Mark's final words to Paul were, "The doctor said my condition is serious, and surgery will be required to save my life. Don't let Denise get away with this." Despite surgery, Mark died later that night from the injuries he sustained when Denise ran into him.

Thereafter, Paul arrested Denise, and on May 24, a Suffolk County grand jury returned an indictment charging Denise with burglary and felony murder.

At Denise's trial, Ann, the owner of Ann's Antiques, testified that on May 20, her store was closed and that

Denise had no right to be in the store. Paul then testified to the pertinent foregoing facts, and began to testify to Mark's statement to him at the hospital. Over the objection of Denise's attorney that Mark's statement to Paul at the hospital constituted inadmissible hearsay, the court (1) permitted Paul to testify to Mark's statement.

When the jury returned a guilty verdict against Denise on the charge of felony murder, her attorney moved to set aside the verdict on the ground that the facts proved at trial failed, as a matter of law, to constitute the crime of felony murder. The court (2) denied the motion.

After the verdict, Jan, a juror, advised Denise's attorney that one afternoon during the trial, she had walked past Ann's Antiques to see for herself whether Paul could really have seen Denise run from the store. Jan said that she thought Paul could have seen Denise, and that while she had discussed her visit to the area with two other jurors during deliberations, the discussion had not affected the jury's verdict. On the basis of Jan's statement, Denise's attorney timely moved for a mistrial. The court (3) denied the motion.

Were the numbered rulings correct?

Now suppose you were sitting for the New York bar exam in July 2001 and ready to answer this question. Following our paradigm, you would begin by reading the interrogatory. Here the call of the question is simply:

"Were the numbered rulings correct?"

As discussed earlier, this type of interrogatory is a common issue-testing technique. However, it is also a common source of difficulty for candidates because the precise issue in controversy is not explicit but rather it is implicit and requires a multi-step analysis to identify it specifically.

Let's outline how you would proceed after completing your reading of the entire fact pattern:

(1) Locate the first ruling in the fact pattern: "The court permitted Paul to testify to Mark's statement."

(2) "Translate" to yourself exactly what the court must have concluded about that statement to allow the testimony.

Here's where legal analysis is required on your part. The issue is not "whether the court was correct in permitting Paul to testify to Mark's statement." This is merely a restatement of the question and not a statement of the issue in controversy.

How do you find the issue? This is the critical step: you must engage in legal analysis and find the controversy behind the ruling by asking yourself:

> *"What is the court's theory in*
> *allowing the testimony?"*

(3) Determine the factual basis for the legal controversy behind the ruling from the fact pattern.

Here you find in the sentence prior to the court ruling that the defense attorney had objected to admission of the statement on the grounds of inadmissible hearsay. Consequently, when the court overruled the objection and permitted the testimony, it had to be because the court found the statement admissible on the basis of an exception to the hearsay rule. Now we have something like:

"The issue is whether the court was correct when it allowed testimony of an out-of-court statement and whether that testimony was admissible based on one of the exceptions to the hearsay rule."

(4) At this point, you have identified an issue suitable for essay writing purposes. However, you should refine it to determine precisely which hearsay exception is in controversy. This ensures that your analysis and articulation of the rule will be on point. As you know, there are many exceptions to the hearsay rule. Your job is not to list and analyze them all; rather, you must focus your discussion on the particular exception raised by the facts of your problem.

(5) To determine the specific hearsay exception, re-read the paragraph which contains Mark's statement. Now the facts will have particular significance to you because you are looking for those facts which fit the elements of a hearsay exception.

You determine that Mark's statement might be considered a dying declaration. This leads to a more complete articulation of the issue:

"The issue is whether the court was correct when it found Mark's statement to be a dying declaration, an exception to the general rule against hearsay, and therefore admissible."

(6) The notes on your outline might look something like this:

Question Two:

(1) General rule: hearsay

Exception: Dying declaration exception according to the New York Rules of Evidence

List the elements required for a dying declaration.

Note: Listing the specific elements of the exception provides an outline to guide your articulation of the rule and application of the facts.

Distinction: Federal Rule/ New York Rule distinction

With some practice, you'll find that your ability to articulate a specific issue from a general statement will become instinctive. Not only is this a valuable skill for the purposes of the exam, but one which you need in practice as well. After all, when your adversary calls out *"Objection!"* during your questioning of a witness, you need to know the basis for the objection in order to refute it.

Question Two contains three rulings. Your outline, therefore, would consist of a list of the rules you need to discuss based on your analysis of the issues. Let's continue our issue analysis to complete a working outline for this question.

For example, the second ruling in Question Two is:

"The court denied the motion."

Once again, you need to read the surrounding sentences to make explicit what the interrogatory provides only implicitly. Applying our technique, we find that:

"The issue is whether the facts proved at trial satisfied all the elements of felony murder."

You can then add to your outline the following:

Question Two:

    (2) Felony murder rule under New York Law

        Underlying felony: facts indicate burglary

            List the elements of burglary as defined in New York

        Distinction: Common law rule of burglary/New York Rule

        Burden of proof:

            On prosecution beyond reasonable doubt

And finally, the court's third ruling is once again:

"The court denied the motion"

which translates to:

"The issue is whether the juror's visit to the crime scene during the trial, unaccompanied by

*the judge, and then discussing the visit with
fellow jurors is the basis for a mistrial."*

Now you can complete your outline and it might
look something like this:

Question Two:

(1) General rule: hearsay

   Exception: Dying declaration exception according to the New York Rules of Evidence

   *List the elements required for a dying
   declaration.*

   Distinction: Federal Rule/ New York Rule
   distinction

(2) Felony murder rule under New York Law

   Underlying felony: facts indicate burglary

   *List the elements of burglary as defined
   in New York*

   Distinction: Common law rule of burglary/New York Rule

   Burden of proof: on prosecution beyond
   reasonable doubt

(3) Basis for mistrial: juror misconduct

   Visiting crime scene unattended

   Premature deliberation/discussions with jurors

   Deliberation with jurors prior to end of
   trial and instructions

As this outline makes clear, each issue forms the basis for a separate IRAC analysis. Further, the outline includes only the rule and its elements or exceptions; there is no need to include facts in your outline. As you write your analysis, you need only work from your articulation of the rule to guide your application of the facts.

b. Finding Issues in the New Jersey Model

February 2002: Question 1

Plaintiff and his friend, Steve, decided to take a bus from the municipally owned and operated Bus Station. As they got to the wooden steps of Bus Station, Steve was distracted and failed to notice a very large hole on the first step that had been there for over a week and had gotten bigger every day. Steve lost his balance when he stepped into this hole. In an effort to steady himself, he reached out for Plaintiff who was next to him. Unfortunately, Plaintiff fell and broke his elbow when Steve grabbed him.

Plaintiff's injury was excruciatingly painful and required the insertion of two metal pins to set the broken bone. Plaintiff did not leave home for three months because of his extreme pain and the limited range of motion in his arm. Within five months of the accident, however, Plaintiff was able to resume all his daily activities. Although the level of pain has subsided, it had not disappeared and was constant.

Plaintiff comes to see you, his attorney, because he wants to sue Bus Station for his injury and would like your written opinion on the merits of all causes of action and all defenses Bus Station could assert.

PREPARE THE OPINION LETTER.

Now suppose you were sitting for the New Jersey bar exam in February 2002 and ready to answer Question 1. Following our paradigm, you would begin by reading the interrogatory. Here the call of the question is more general than the New York Model. Even a quick reading of this interrogatory tells you what you are looking for: all causes of action and possible defenses. You can use the bifurcation in the question to set up your outline which should look something like this:

(1) Plaintiff's possible causes of action

(2) Bus Station's possible defenses

If you leave adequate space, you can list the appropriate legal theories as you find them in the fact pattern. For example, your subsequent reading of this problem might yield an outline that looks something like the following:

(1) Plaintiff's possible causes of action

   Negligence:

      Duty:

         Duty owed to an invitee; common carrier serving the public

      Breach:

         Left large hole for over a week

      Legal cause:

         "But for" the hole/ failure to repair

      Proximate cause:

         Foreseeability of passenger injury from failure to properly maintain premises

      Damages

(2) Bus Station's possible defenses

Contributory/Comparative negligence

Governmental immunity from suit

The secret to writing a successful answer for this type of essay is to organize your response. Use subheadings to separate the "causes of action" from the "possible defenses." While it may appear easier to answer this type of question as opposed to the New York model where you have to engage in some preliminary deduction to find the issue, you must be careful nonetheless to keep your analysis on-point and fact-driven. The issue may well be whether the Bus Station was negligent but its negligence occurred within a particular set of circumstances. Your ability to keep your response tied to the facts of the problem will ensure that you complete your analysis in a focused and timely manner.

This approach is appropriate for those questions which follow the New Jersey model, despite variations in length and format. Whether the candidate must evaluate alternative courses of conduct, select among competing arguments, or advise a client as to the viability of various causes of action, the need to structure these discussions around the issues and sub-issues remains constant.

c. *Practicing the Principle*

The Connecticut bar exam essays offer an excellent illustration of this principle. While Connecticut

essays follow the New Jersey model, they are somewhat shorter. Not to worry, however, Connecticut
compensates by having more of them since the
Connecticut candidate will have twelve essays to
complete! Nonetheless, the candidate must be very
careful to work from an issue-based analysis and
keep focused or face the very real likelihood of not
completing all of the questions.

As the following example makes clear, while a
question may be shorter, it nonetheless requires a
complete and thoughtful analysis based on an identification of the relevant issues. The difference is
that there are fewer principle points of law to
discuss.

Connecticut Bar Examination, July 2000

Question 2

The city of Nice maintains a website to which per-
sons or entities can submit items for posting. There are
numerous categories including, among other things,
coming events, op-ed pieces, and times and locations of
religious services. If a submission fits within one of the
site's many categories and complies with the criteria for
that category, it will be posted.

Another one of the categories is "What's On At The
Movies?" which regularly posts the names of the movies playing at area cinemas, their ratings and their
show times. The site rejected that part of a submission
by Big Mall Multiplex which referred to a recent re-
make of Lady Chatterly's Lover, a movie based on a
novel of the same name by D.H. Lawrence, because the

movie's rating is "X" and the site will not list X-rated movies.

Big Mall Multiplex has filed a Section 42 USC 1983 action against the City of Nice, seeking declaratory and injunctive relief. Thoroughly analyze the constitutional issues that Big Mall Multiplex can raise in its action.

This question poses the typical problem for the bar candidate: how to complete a concise and thorough analysis in a timely manner of what is arguably an open-ended, amorphous question dealing with "constitutional issues." In such instances, the candidate must remain as faithful to articulating the "issue" as the candidate in the jurisdiction where the interrogatory poses a narrow and particular question.

Let's see how you would think through this question to find the appropriate constitutional issues:

(1) Begin by asking yourself which constitutional right was infringed when Big Mall's submission was rejected for posting on the city's website.

  (a) Isolate the significant acts and facts: "posting on a website," "coming events," "op-ed pieces", "movie listings," and "times and locations of religious services."

  (b) Using these facts, engage in a kind of free association: ask yourself, "what are these about?" Answer: they're about a website but it's acting like a newspaper where parties can "post" or "publish" on it. Here, Big Mall is being denied the right to post information. What constitutional issue does publishing in a "newspaper" implicate?

(2) By focusing on the facts, you're led to what might be an infringement on Big Mall's First Amendment's freedom of speech.

(3) From here, you need to start thinking about the sub-issues involved in a freedom of speech analysis. You would start with the general questions and then work to refine them.

   (a) Who is regulating whom?

   (b) What kind of speech is being regulated?

(4) Now you have the two main principles of law based on the issues that you can use to frame your outline: standing and commercial speech.

F. WRITING THE ESSAY

Now that you've framed an outline based on the rules which address the issues raised in the question, you're ready to write your analysis. But first take a moment to re-read the interrogatory and make sure that your outline addresses each of the questions asked.

The actual essay will follow one of two general formats: first, where you are asked to assume a role and evaluate alternative courses of action or discuss all the relevant issues; and second, where you are asked to come to only one conclusion.

In either case, your goal is the same: to answer the question with a solid analysis of the relevant rule and facts. You're not writing to impress the grader—the grader already has all the answers but must find out whether *you* know the answers. Provide them by working through a basic IRAC analysis. Never shy away from stating the obvious when it's "obviously" what's asked of you. As I've said before, the questions on the bar exam are designed to test your ability to engage in basic legal analysis.

"Where You're Asked to Assume a Role"

Some jurisdictions ask you to assume a particular role or write in a particular format. For example, you might be asked to pretend that you're the prosecutor, the defense attorney, or the law clerk. Similarly, you might be asked to draft a client letter, an opinion letter, or a memorandum. In these instances, you want to adopt the appropriate tone and point of view in your writing and use an acceptable format.

Assume that you're asked to write a client letter. You should start your answer with something like,

"Dear Client,

After a careful review of the circumstances of your injury, I believe that you might assert the following causes of action: ...... "

Alternatively, you may be asked to write a memorandum posing as a law clerk to a judge or a partner in a law firm. In this case, your response might look like this:

TO:	Judge (add name if given); Senior Partner
FROM:	Law clerk
RE:	Chargeable offenses in *State v. Jones*
or	Available remedies in *Smith v. Jones* breach of contract action

While it's important that you assume the role the bar examiners have asked you to play because it shows you have read the question carefully and followed the directions, you should not craft elaborate, fictitious letterheads or memo headings. This would be a waste of your valuable time and would not yield additional points.

As discussed throughout this book, the model format for writing exam answers is IRAC—or some variation of it. Consequently, after the appropriate introduction, you should begin your analysis with a brief statement of the issue. Even where the questions are general in that you are identifying possible causes of action or assessing the admissibility of evidence, you should still identify an issue. The issue might be whether the facts support a cause of action in battery, assault, or intentional infliction of emotional distress; similarly, the issue might be whether the business records exception is appropriate to allow admission of otherwise inadmissible hearsay statements, or whether offers to pay medical expenses are admissible. A statement of the issue is vital for two reasons: first, it informs your reader, in this case your very-important grader, that you have identified the legal controversy in the facts; and second, it leads you to the statement of the rule needed to resolve that controversy.

After articulation of the issue, the structure for writing exam essays is virtually identical. Accordingly, you can refer to the following section on conclusion-based essays and proceed to the section on writing the rule.

"Where You're Required to Reach a Single Conclusion"

In those jurisdictions where you're asked to come to a resolution, you will need to identify a conclusion or set of conclusions. However, while you must reach a conclusion, the actual conclusion is not the goal of the essay. The bar examiners are not interested in the bottom line result but in the line of reasoning you followed to reach that result. In fact, as you review released bar exam essays, you will find sample answers that reach opposite conclusions as to the identical issue! Clearly, the bar examiners are sending you a message by their choice: it is not the conclusion but the logic of your reasoning that counts.

1.   Writing the Conclusion (where required)

The difficulty with this form of essay question is that you won't know your conclusion until you've completed a thorough analysis of the problem. It's simply impossible to come to any resolution before then. Nor is it necessary. Simply leave several lines at the beginning of your response and fill them in after you've completed your analysis.

Your answer to this type of question might look something like this:

Question One

Conclusions:

(1)

(2)

(3)

Analysis:

(1)

Not only does this set forth an organized, easy-to-follow format for the grader to follow in reading your essay, but it provides you with a starting point and structure. The actual writing of the conclusion is a simple affair: it is a one sentence statement that answers the question raised in the interrogatory. It might be something like:

"The Defendant can be found guilty of felony murder based on his commission of the underlying felony of burglary."

In these "CIRAC" jurisdictions, you will write the conclusion yet again at the end of your analysis. This is to provide a logical end to your discussion and in effect does nothing more than reiterate the conclusion you reached earlier.

2. Writing the Issue

Where the bar examiners ask a specific question which requires identification of the legal issue in controversy, points are generally allocated for a statement of the issue.

Let's identify some rules for writing effective statements of the issue:

(1) Begin your sentence with *"The issue is whether."* It's okay to be obvious. There's no need to worry that you're boring the grader. He or she will be very grateful to find the issue in your essay so easily. Also, there's no need to try and impress the grader with your originality. Save the sparkling prose for your law review articles and proceed swiftly through your paces on the bar.

(2) Narrow the issue to the facts in question.

Thus, an issue is not a general statement like,

"The issue is whether the court was correct in denying the motion."

Instead, you need to identify the legal question as to why granting the motion might be in controversy such as:

"The issue is whether the statement was hearsay and whether it fit within any exception permitting its admission at trial."

(3) Avoid overly general issue statements. An issue is rarely if ever such a general statement as:

"The issue is whether there was a contract."

Instead, look to identify the facts which make it questionable whether a contract was formed:

"The issue is whether a contract was formed *when* the acceptance stated additional terms."

Or

"The issue is whether the buyer can enforce its requirements contract with the seller *when* the buyer doubled its requirements after two months."

A key to both finding and writing the issue is to use the word "when" because it forces you to focus on the facts in the problem.

The identification of issues takes some practice but is well worth the result: you get points on your essay because you show the grader that you've recognized the legal problem raised by the facts.

3. Writing the Rule of Law

After your identification of the issue, your statement of the rule of law is probably the single most important part of your exam essay. First, it lets the reader know that you have identified the legal problem and second, it shows that you know the relevant law. The major problem, and where candidates fail to get as many points as they can and should, is that they do not write enough law and they do not do it in a complete, concise, and coherent manner.

The general rule about writing the rule is to write enough law to provide the context in which you will analyze the facts. The rule and the facts are inextricably linked. Your analysis of the facts will not make sense unless you have first identified the rule which determines the relevance of those facts. You must use the facts of the problem to guide your discussion of the law.

Let's break this down into two steps: first, writing enough of the rule, and second, writing the rule in a logical order.

a.   Write enough rule

By now I'm sure you're asking yourself:

- What is enough rule?

- How do I know how much rule to write?

- Isn't there such a thing as too much rule?

The answer is simple: the whole rule is enough rule to provide the context for which you will analyze the facts.

For example, if your issue calls for a discussion of contract formation, a sentence such as, "A valid contract requires an offer, an acceptance, and consideration" would be insufficient as your entire statement of the rule of law. Regrettably, this is very often the only sentence a candidate will write regarding the rule of law before moving on to an equally cryptic discussion of the facts. What's missing is a definition of each of the legal terms of art raised in the statement of law: What constitutes a "valid offer," what qualifies as an "acceptance," and what is a "bargained for exchange"?

Similarly, a candidate's incomplete statement of the rule for an analysis of a battery problem might read something like this:

"A battery is the intentional infliction of a harmful or offensive bodily contact."

Here, a relevant discussion of the legal meaning of intent is completely absent. As you know from your first year torts class, the concept of intent is critical when analyzing any of the intentional torts. Also absent is an adequate explanation of what constitutes a "harmful or offensive" contact. Accordingly, you can imagine the grader looking at the scoring checklist and wondering where something like the following statement of the rule was to be found:

"A battery is the intentional infliction of a harmful or offensive bodily contact. In order to prove intent for battery, one must prove either that the defendant intended to bring about the wrongful physical contact with the person of another or cause an imminent apprehension of such a contact, or that the defendant knew with substantial certainty that his or her conduct would result in physical consequences. A harmful contact is one which causes pain or bodily injury. An offensive contact is one that is offensive or damaging to a reasonable person's sense of dignity. Further, the plaintiff need not have actual awareness of the contact, which may be direct or indirect, at the time it occurs in order for a battery to result."

After reading this paragraph, you should realize that the sentence—"a battery is the intentional infliction of a harmful or offensive bodily contact"— would be only the first sentence in your statement of the relevant law. You should also realize that it would be a very important sentence because it forms the foundation from which you will build the rule of law.

The procedure for constructing a solid statement of the rule of law is as follows:

1.   Read the interrogatory for the call-of-the-question.

2.   Typically, your first response to the interrogatory after you've read the entire hypothetical will be the specific rule, element, or exception to the general rule needed to answer the question.

For example, when you read a question in the context of a sales hypothetical that asks:

"Whether Seller's non-conforming delivery afforded Buyer the right to cancel"

there is a very strong likelihood that you will immediately form an answer that concludes something like this:

"No, Buyer does not have the right to cancel when Seller has the right to cure the non-conformity because the time for performance is not yet due."

With this response, you've identified the very narrow rule of law you need to answer the specific legal question.

3.   Write "the right to cure" in your rule outline. This is your first block in building the rule of law.

4. Now think backward and then forward to fill out the whole rule by evaluating and applying the essential building blocks for rule construction.

Consider the following:

(a) *Elements of rules*: If you've identified a specific element of a rule as relevant to your problem, then go back and begin with a general statement identifying all of the elements.

Suppose your question raises a negligence issue with respect to the duty of care based on the nature of the parties' relationship. While the primary focus of your legal discussion will be centered on the standard of care and whether or not it was breached, you will preface your analysis with a general statement identifying the basic elements required for a cause of action in negligence: duty, breach, cause-in-fact, proximate cause, and injury.

Similarly, assume your question requires an analysis of the enforceability of a restrictive employment covenant where your answer to the interrogatory turns specifically on one of the covenant's provisions, you will nonetheless identify all of the factors the courts look to in assessing such agreements.

(b) *Definitions*: You can build on your general statement of law by writing a definition for each of the legal terms of art you've identified. A basic definition can be written in a sentence or two. What you must do is avoid going beyond the scope of the question and writing a treatise on rules not in controversy. Let the facts of the problem be your guide and do not stray from them.

(c) *Exceptions to the general rule*: If, on the other hand, you have identified an exception to a general rule as the critical factor for your problem, then go back and identify the general rule. A statement of the general rule provides a much-needed context for understanding the exception.

A good example of where you would work backward from the exception to the general rule would be questions that test the Fourth Amendment's prohibition against unreasonable searches and seizures and its corollary, the exclusionary rule. The many exceptions to the Fourth Amendment make it a fertile field for bar examiners. Another example would be evidence questions dealing with hearsay issues. Just think of all the possible exceptions to the hearsay rule! Of course such essay questions are not limited to the Fourth Amendment and the hearsay rule. Given the nature of the law, the list is practically endless: when is there not an exception to a rule? All this means is that when your task is to analyze an exception, you want to begin that discussion with a statement of the general rule before you turn your attention to the specific exception brought into controversy by the facts of your problem.

The following are some examples that illustrate the process of building the rule of law by moving from the general rule to the exception and defining legal terms of art. The selections are from actual student answers chosen by the New York Board of Law Examiners as samples of above average candidate answers. Note, however, that the Board is careful to make no representation as to the accuracy of the answers; they are simply considered above average responses. This is important to remember as you review sample answers so that you do not rely on them as your source of the substantive law.

Fourth Amendment issue:

New York State Bar Examination, February 2002

Question 2, Sample Answer 1

"Under the 4th Amendment, a person has the right to be free from unlawful search and seizures by the government. Seizure under the 4th Amendment includes arrests. For an arrest to be proper under the 4th Amendment it must be made pursuant to a warrant unless it is conducted in a public place and the police officer has probable cause (information sufficient that a reasonably prudent person would believe that the suspect committed the crime). A stop of a vehicle may be conducted properly so long as the police have some reasonable and articulable reason for the stop. The reasonable suspicion required for a valid stop does not have to rise to the level of probable cause."

Hearsay issue:

New York State Bar Examination, July 2001

Question 2, Sample Answer 2

"Under the New York rules of evidence, hearsay is an out of court statement offered for the truth of the matter asserted. Hearsay is inadmissible unless it falls within an exception or is excluded from the definition of hearsay. A "dying declaration" is an exception to the rule against hearsay and may be admitted for the purposes of establishing its truth. In order to be admissible, the statement must be made 1) under a sense of impending death, 2) it must concern the circumstances that put the declarant in the position of impending death, 3) the declarant must thereafter die, 4) the declarant must have been competent to testify at trial, and 5) in New York, the exception may only be used in a homicide case."

Seller's "right to cure" issue:

New York State Bar Examination, July 2001

Question 1, Sample Answer 2

"The general rule for buyer's rights on receipt of non-conforming goods is that a buyer may reject the goods entirely, retain units that conform to the contract, or accept the non-conforming goods. However, there is an exception to the general rule when a seller ships non-conforming goods before performance is due. In this case, a seller may notify the buyer upon learning of the non-conformity of its intent to cure. The buyer must accept conforming goods tendered when performance is due and may not cancel the contract before then."

> Note: Remember, your reasoning process would begin with the exception and you'd work your way back to the general rule. This is why your outline is so important. It lets you put the rule in order before you write.

(d) *Distinctions*: Look for distinctions between the law of your jurisdiction and the federal law and where the common law differs from statutory law. These are some of the bar examiners' favorite exam issues because they test your knowledge and understanding of the law. A knowledgeable candidate will note such distinctions to demonstrate his or her understanding of how application of one rule as opposed to the other will yield a different result.

The following are some noteworthy examples of distinctions between state and federal and common law and statutory law. They show how you can demonstrate your grasp and understanding of critical nuances in the law—and gain points from your grader—with just an additional sentence or two in your answer. As you prepare for the bar, make note of such exceptions and look for them on exam day.

The "Dying Declaration" distinction:

Under the Federal Rules of Evidence, a statement made under the belief of impending death concerning what the declarant believed to be the circumstances of his impending death is admissible in a prosecution for homicide or in a civil action. FRE 804(b)(2). Unlike the federal rule, however, such testimony is admissible in New York only if the declarant dies and the death is the subject of a homicide charge.

The common law's "mirror image rule" and the UCC:

Under the common law, the "mirror image rule" requires that an acceptance conform exactly to the terms of the offer and any variation is deemed a counter-offer and terminates the offeree's power of acceptance. The result under the UCC is radically different. Here, a contract for the sale of goods may occur even if the acceptance contains terms additional to or different from the offer. Consequently, in one case we have a contract whereas in the other we don't.

An important caveat when writing the rule:

Don't waste time discussing issues that are not in controversy. If, for example, the question tells you that the **will was duly executed,** you don't need to spend time identifying the rules for execution. Obviously, the issue in controversy was not the validity of the execution but some other issue. A similar example is when you're told there was **proper service of process**. Once again, there is no need to discuss the issue of service and how it was effected in this case. The bar examiners are telling you in language as plain as they can make it that these are not the issues in the question. If you choose to ignore such signals, not only do you waste your valuable time while not adding to your point score, but you are telling the grader that you've not read the question carefully—a double "no-no." Don't do it!

b.　*Write the rule in its logical order*

There is a structure to follow when writing a rule of law. You should strive to present your statement of the law in its logical order. This demonstrates your understanding of the subject and makes it clear to the grader.

Consider the following hierarchy of concepts when you draft your rule outline:

● Move from the general to the specific.

Your analysis should begin with a statement of the general rule and move to the exception. This is simply the natural order of things.

● Define each legal term of art.

When your statement of the rule contains a legal term of art, your next sentence should be a definition of that term. This is one of the easiest ways to go about building a complete statement of the rule in a logical and methodical manner. The sentences flow without effort because one statement leads naturally to the next.

Excerpt from New York State Bar Examination, July 2000

Question 1, Excerpt from Sample Answer 1

Note: This question required an analysis of a buyer's claim for damages when the buyer has inspected and accepted delivery of goods which subsequently fail to perform as warranted.

". . . contracts for the sale of goods often contain express and implied warranties. An express warranty is one that is given by a merchant (one specializing in the sale of particular goods) as to a specific quality that the goods have. An express warranty cannot be waived by a purchaser. An implied warranty of merchantability is created between parties when a seller typically deals in a certain type of goods and sells those goods. In the sale, there is an implied warranty of merchantability that the goods are fit for their ordinary purpose. An implied warranty of merchantability can be waived either expressly through language (i.e. "as is") or through conduct. Finally, an implied warranty of fitness arises when a merchant sells products which he knows the buyer relies on his opinion, and those products are to be used for a specific purpose of which the seller knows. An implied warranty of fitness can also be waived through conspicuous language or through waiver by the buyer if certain fitness defects can be reasonably discovered upon inspection by the buyer."

4. Writing the Application

The application portion of your essay is just that—an analysis of the facts. It is not a recitation of the facts. The grader will not give you credit for merely restating the facts in the problem. Rather, your job is to examine the legal significance of each fact in light of the rule of law.

Regrettably, however, too many bar candidates skip right over the application in their haste to reach a conclusion. Not only do they sacrifice valuable points, but they give up some of the easiest points to get. First, the facts are given to you in the hypothetical. You don't need to rely on your memory as you must for reciting the law. Second, you've already completed the difficult part of your job when you found the legal issue. Now you just need to follow through by matching up each element or definition from the rule with the appropriate fact.

There are two key words to guide your writing of the application. Using these words will ensure that what you write is "analysis" and not "recitation."

a. Use signal words

Use the word *"Here"* to introduce your application. This word acts as a signal to the reader, letting him or her know that you've moved from your statements of rule to the specifics of the problem. When you get bored, you can always use *"In this case"* but as I've told you before, there's little need to worry about boring your reader. Whatever you do to make your reader's job easier by providing clear transitions will be greatly appreciated.

b. The importance of "because"

Use the word *"Because"* to draw the connection between rule and fact. "Because" is the single most important word to use when writing your application. It is also a signal word—but more for your benefit than the grader. Using the word "because" forces you to make the connection between rule and fact.

For example, many a bar candidate overlooks the obvious statement,

"This was a contract for the sales of goods because computers are goods,"

but such a sentence is essential to a solid analysis because it completes the nexus between your statement of law that the Uniform Commercial Code governs transactions involving sales of goods and your facts which discuss the sale and delivery of computers.

5.　Stating or Restating the Conclusion

After you've completed your application of the facts to the rules, either state or restate your conclusion, as appropriate. This provides a logical close to your argument. Once again, you can rely on a signal word to mark your transition: "***Therefore***, it is likely that a partnership will be found," " . . . a contract was formed," " . . . an injunction will be granted."

G.　FOLLOW THE FORMULA

To summarize what we've just discussed at great length, the secret to writing successful bar exam essays is to organize them around each issue and its concomitant rule of law. You should write a separate paragraph for each rule which forms its own mini-IRAC. The composition of the paragraph is well-defined. Following this structure leads you through the thought process, albeit in a mechanical manner, but until it becomes habit, it nonetheless produces the desired result: a legal analysis that goes through all the steps in a comprehensible, organized manner!

Still, this formula is meant only as a guide to ensure that you follow the structure of sound legal analysis; certainly, it is not the only way to write a bar exam answer. Ideally, after your articulation of the issue, your discussion should be a seamless web of law and fact. A number of sample answers you will read will be written like this and if this is your style, by all means continue to write in such a manner.

If you rely on the formula, however, the construction of your paragraph might read something like this:

Sentence one is the issue statement:

"The issue is whether . . . ."

> "The issue is whether an employer is entitled to a preliminary injunction **when** his former employee breaches a non-compete clause that results in minimal loss to the employer."

Sentence two (or more) provides the rule:

"Under the [state the controlling law: common law, federal rule, state-specific statute etc.],

> "Under the New York Civil Practice Law and Rules ("CPLR"), a preliminary injunction is a

provisional remedy available when the moving party shows that he would have a reasonable likelihood of success on the merits, that if an injunction were denied he would suffer irreparable harm which would be hard to measure with money damages, and that the balance of equities favors him."

Sentence three (or so) is the application:

"**Here**, the [parties . . . .]."

"Here the employer is not likely to be granted a preliminary injunction because he has not shown that the terms of the agreement were enforceable and that he would likely succeed in the underlying action; second, he has not shown that he faces irreparable harm as a result of the employee's working for a competitor because he has not lost any of his customers to that competitor and third, he has not shown that the employee's leaving was responsible for customer loss in any way."

Sentence four (or so) is the conclusion:

"**Therefore**,

"Therefore, the employer will not be successful in obtaining a preliminary injunction."

Conversely, if you prefer to weave together law and fact, the following excerpts from sample answer 2 for Question 1 of the February 1998 New York Bar Exam provide a good example:

Excerpt 1:

Even though a contract may specify a closing date, this time for performance may be changed if requested by one of the parties unless "time has been made of the essence." This contract did not do so. Thus, Purch could request a later date for performance.

Sid responded to Purch's request for an extension in writing at which time Sid made the new date, which Purch himself had selected, to be of the *essence*. Courts in New York will allow time to be made of the essence where the time set for performance is reasonable (Purch set the new date which was over five weeks from the original date), there is notice given (Sid's notice was in writing), and it is clear and unequivocal that time is now of the essence (Sid informed Purch he would hold him in default if he did not appear).

Excerpt 2:

While Sid had at first been an at-will employee which in New York means that an employer may terminate that employee for any reason or no reason, upon his employment with Doc, Sid signed a non-compete agreement. These agreements are closely scrutinized because they limit an employee's ability to seek future employment and act as a restraint on trade. New York courts will look to the following factors in assessing such agreements:

(1) The scope of the agreement—this refers to the geographic limits of the agreement and whether it was reasonable.

(2) The duration—how long a period of time the employee will be restricted.

(3) The employee's services and whether they were special, unique or extraordinary.

In this instance, Sid signed an agreement without much choice since he needed to support his family and one might argue he was not on equal bargaining terms with Doc. In any event, the agreement limited him from employment as a doctor for three years following a dismissal with or without cause. Three years might well be considered too long a restriction to be upheld.

Sid was also restricted from practicing in the entire city of Glens Falls. This too seems unreasonable since there are 15,000 citizens in the city. While Sid is a doctor and doctors like to think their services are unique, extraordinary and special, Sid was not a particular specialist and to be denied pursuit of his livelihood for three years anywhere in the city could well be unreasonable.

Whether your writing style follows the paragraph paradigm or weaves rule and fact together, your goal remains the same: present a well-reasoned, structured analysis of the issue in a lawyer-like manner.

H. PRACTICE MAKES POINTS

1. Gaining Familiarity with the Questions

The key to success in any endeavor is preparation. Familiarity with the structure of the essay questions and how you respond to them will go a long way in alleviating your anxiety on test day. You job is to practice the approach we've just outlined so that it becomes so automatic by test day that you move from one step to the other without missing a beat.

The difficulty, of course, is finding the time to practice these skills. Finding time will be one of your greatest challenges during the bar review period. You'll be torn in several directions at once—going to bar review lectures, reviewing your notes, memorizing the law, writing essays, answering multiple choice questions, and taking simulated MPT exams. Still, there are ways to ensure that you accomplish all that you must. Once again, it comes down to knowing your own strengths and weaknesses and working with them.

A bit of common sense goes a long way. If you have solid writing skills and law school essays were your strong point, then there may be no need to write out complete essay answers. Instead, what you will do is focus on identifying issues and outlining the rules needed to address those issues. You should aim to outline at least two bar examination essays every day during your two month bar prep period. Pay particular attention to articulating the issues. As you've learned by now, it takes skill to move from the interrogatory or general question to the specific issue in controversy. Only sufficient practice will enable you to articulate issues with ease. Outline all of the essay questions available from your jurisdiction, then move on to the essays from your bar review course.

On the other hand, if writing was not one of your strengths, you must write complete essay answers. It will not be sufficient for you to merely outline the rules according to the issues; you need to practice writing according to the outlined formula until it becomes automatic and the words flow from your pen. There is no short cut. The key to building your

confidence, your competence, and your efficiency
will come only from practice, practice, and more
practice.

2.   Working with Sample Answers

Finally, whether you've written out entire essays
or only outlined the issues and rules, be sure to
read the sample answers. Read all of them, even
when there are several candidate samples for each
question. For example, New York provides two candidate answers whenever possible, as does New
Jersey. On the other hand, Connecticut gives seven
sample answers for each question, providing the
applicant with an opportunity to see a range of
scores. Connecticut's bar examiners identify the
scoring system and you can read for yourself what
was considered a "much below average" response
as opposed to a "much above average" response,
and everything in between.

Reading selected candidate answers is an excellent way to become familiar with the predilections
of your jurisdiction. However, be careful to read
with a discerning eye toward the rules of law ex-
pressed in student papers: the bar examiners are
careful to point out that they are only "sample"
answers, not "model" answers. Consequently, you
may find what you consider errors in statements of
the law. Use this to your advantage: if you're reading the answers "actively" as indeed you should be,
then you will identify these errors and be sure to
articulate the correct rule of law. Further, you

should compare each sample answer to the IRAC model and fully analyze the construction. Then you should compare the sample to your own answer, element by element, taking the time to evaluate what you've written. To truly benefit from the sample answers, it's not enough to skim through them: you must de-construct them using forensic IRAC.

I. USING FORENSIC IRAC TO DIAG-NOSE YOUR ESSAYS

1.   Becoming Your Own Grader

Let's face it: the ideal situation would be to have a *bona fide* bar examination grader beside you to evaluate your essays as you write them. You'd have instant feedback from someone who knows how these essays should be written and could tell you what you've done right and where you've gone wrong. The bad news is that we both know this is not about to happen. The good news is that you can develop the ability to do this kind of assessment for yourself. All you need are the right tools. And, like Dorothy in the Wizard of Oz who had the means to return home all the time, you too have exactly what you need to be your own guide. By learning to apply forensic IRAC to your own essays, you'll be able to identify the flaws in your legal analysis and correct them. In effect, you'll become your own personal grader but with one significant advantage: you'll be able to change the outcome!

2. How It Works

As you've learned in this chapter, an effective essay follows the IRAC structure. As a result, your essays should include an "issue," a "rule," an "application," and a "conclusion." Once you've written the essay, you have all the evidence you need to use our forensic principles. By examining what you've written through the legal lens of IRAC, you'll be able to evaluate your own work.

Clearly the first step in this process is to write an essay. Assuming that you've written an essay answer during one of your practice sessions, the next step is to put it away. Move on to something else— review your lecture notes, prepare some flash cards, write another essay. You're not ready to be objective about something you've just completed. You're too close to see what you've *really* written as opposed to what you *think* you've written. The mind's eye is funny that way: you can read something you've written over and over again and never see the errors because your eye will correct them based on what your mind intended. The only way to overcome this tendency is to distance yourself from your work so you can look at what you've written with a fresh eye and a clear mind. I strongly recommend that you write an essay one day and review it the next.

Sometime the next day, or much, much later that same day, take out the bar exam question and your essay. Re-read the question and then your answer. Now you're ready to proceed. The plan is simple:

use IRAC analysis to detect any flaws in that analysis.

What follows is a step-by-step guide for performing a self-diagnostic on your essay. It works by examining what you've written to reveal your thought process. It's like deciphering a code, where each sentence is a clue in piecing together how you approached the problem. What you've written leaves an identifiable trail—something like your DNA but instead identifying your biologic self, it identifies your cognitive self.

As you read your essay, consider each IRAC element against the criteria outlined below. This allows you to evaluate what you've written with the critical eye of a grader and identify your individual strengths and weaknesses. More importantly, by showing you exactly what to look for in each step of an IRAC analysis, you'll be able to pinpoint exactly where in the process any weakness occurs. Then, by following the suggested cures for that particular problem, you'll be able to correct it.

J. IRAC SELF–DIAGNOSTIC FOR ESSAYS

1.   When the "Issue" is the Problem

a.   *How you can tell*

Generally, you can spot a problem with the "issue" by what's written in the application. A failure to identify an issue manifests itself in what the New Jersey Board of Bar Examiners referred to as a "scattershot" application. In these cases, the discussion rambles and roams, moving without any logical transition from topic to topic. Unfortunately, the writer's initial failure to identify the legal question leads to a circular narrative which tends to go on and on. What's interesting however, is that a knowledge of substantive law is indicated but since what is written doesn't connect with what is asked, the points gained are very few.

You can also find evidence of an issue problem in the statement of the rule. These are slightly more difficult situations to assess because there's an apparent discussion of the law and some factual discussion but once again, it is not "on point" or more precisely, on "any point." There may even be an opening *"The issue is whether"* statement, but it merely restates the interrogatory without articulating the legal question underlying it. As a result, you're misled into thinking you've identified the issue while in fact you've missed it altogether.

Look for examples of the following in the application:

☐ No clear theme or focus.

☐ No connection between the fact pattern's interrogatory and the written answer.

☐ A rambling and repetitious narrative.

Look for examples of the following in the rule:

☐ A lengthy, treatise-like approach to general legal topics.

☐ Short declarative statements of general legal concepts, without further legal discussion. For example:

- "A contract requires offer, acceptance, and consideration."

- "Hearsay is an out-of-court statement asserted to prove the truth of the matter asserted."

- "Corporate officers and directors of a corporation owe a duty of loyalty to the corporation."

- "Every partner is an agent of the partnership for the purpose of its business."

b. How you can cure

☐ Begin your analysis by identifying the type of interrogatory.

Does it follow the New York model?

- Was the court correct in granting the motion for summary judgment?

- Can the defendant successfully assert the defense of justification?

- Were the numbered rulings correct?

Does it follow the New Jersey model?

- Discuss the rights and liabilities of all parties.

- Discuss all causes of action.

- Analyze fully.

☐ Articulate the issue based on the interrogatory.

- *For the New York model*: identify the legal controversy behind the ruling/defense/argument by asking yourself: *what is the theory behind this position?*

Let's look at an interrogatory from Question 1 of the February 2000 exam:

"Did RM have the right to terminate its agreement with Dave?"

Do not write as your statement of the issue:

"The issue is whether RM had a right to terminate its agreement with Dave."

This is merely a restatement of the interrogatory.

Instead, you need to review the facts to determine what about the parties' agreement might allow for a termination. After reading the facts, it becomes clear that the legal controversy is:

"The issue is whether the parties' contract containing a termination provision was valid."

By identifying the legal issue as one concerning the enforceability of a termination provision, your subsequent discussion of the rule will include more than just *"A valid contract requires an offer, an acceptance, and consideration."* Rather, you'll recognize the need to discuss the validity of contract terms and whether this one-sided termination provision was the result of a bargained-for exchange.

- *For the New Jersey model*: identify the nature of your task. Determine whether you need to identity causes of action, possible defenses, or courses of conduct.

☐ Develop your outline according to the issue.

For the New York model:

- Each issue forms the basis for a separate IRAC analysis.

- Outline only the rule and its elements or exceptions.

- As you write your analysis, work only from your articulation of the rule to guide your application of the facts.

For the New Jersey model:

- Use subheadings to organize your response.

- Structure discussions around the issues and sub-issues.

2. When the "Rule" is the Problem

There are two separate and distinct problems which can show up in the "rule" portion of the analysis: first, where there is a genuine ignorance of the law; and, second, where there's a demonstration of substantive knowledge, but it's sketchy and incomplete. Here there's not "enough" rule to provide an adequate context for analyzing the facts.

(1) Where there's ignorance of the applicable rule

a. *How you can tell*

Look for examples of the following in the "rule" section:

☐ Statements that smack of legalese but state nothing substantive.

☐ General discussion without legal terminology, thus sounding as if written by a non-lawyer.

☐ Misstatements of the law.

☐ Illogical, disjointed statements of the rule.

☐ A lack of a hierarchical structure to the rules and sub-rules.

Look for examples of the following in the "application" section:

☐ Repetition of the facts with no analysis.

☐ Inconsistent statements.

☐ No distinction between relevant and irrelevant facts.

☐ No connection between a fact and its legal significance.

b. *How you can cure*

As you well know, there are a number of reasons why you don't know something. The most obvious reason is that you simply didn't spend enough time studying and memorizing the black letter law. On the other hand, a lack of knowledge can result from an inability to integrate and learn legal principles. Sometimes, you may spend adequate time in study but the time is ineffective for any number of reasons.

In this case, the cure requires that you take a different approach in your studying. In addition to reviewing your notes and memorizing black letter law, you are going to integrate the following tasks into your study plan:

- Re-write rules of law in your own words.

  Put the parts/elements of rules together in a way that forms a logical whole. Memorize them.

- Having memorized rules, make sure you understand how to apply them to new fact situations. Practice applying the rules to hypotheticals. Answer objective, multiple choice questions in that area of the law.

- Practice turning rules into issues and questions. Don't stop at memorizing the definition of an "offer." Learn to ask yourself, "what do I need to ask to determine whether a valid offer was made?"

  (2) Where there's knowledge of the rule but it's absent or insufficient.

Interestingly, a problem of this nature reveals itself in the "application" portion of the essay. Here the discussion analyzes the facts but without first providing the context of law to make that discussion meaningful. Clearly, the candidate relied on legal knowledge to write the application because without such knowledge and recognition of the relevant law, there could have been no meaningful analysis.

a. *How you can tell*

Look for examples of the following in the "application" section:

☐ Solid factual discussion that is element-based but without any explanation/identification of the element.

☐ Analysis of the legally-relevant facts but without discussion of the relevant law.

  b.   How you can cure

☐ Build your legal context by working backwards from the facts to determine the scope of the rule necessary to lay a foundation for the subsequent discussion of the facts.

☐ Follow the building block approach to construct your rule of law:

  ☐ Do you need to list the *elements* in your rule?

  ☐ Do you need to *define* legal terms?

  ☐ Is there a *general rule* that provides the context for the exception?

  ☐ Are there any *federal/state distinctions* or *common law/statutory law distinctions* you need to identify?

  3.   When the "Application" is the Problem

This is by far the simplest problem to correct because the essay has the rules in place but fails to analyze the facts. Clearly, the writer implicitly acknowledged the relevance of the facts or he or she would not have recognized the need to discuss that rule.

  a.   How you can tell

☐ Mere repetition of the facts from the hypothetical.

☐ Conclusory statements.

☐ Use of such language as "obviously," "clearly," and "evidently."

b. How you can cure

☐ Match up each element/sub-element in the rule to a fact.

☐ Use the word "because" to make the connection between rule and fact.

☐ Make sure that every conclusion you reach is supported by an explanation of the "why" behind it.

K. OTHER ESSAY WRITING TECHNIQUES

1. Use sub-headings to keep answers organized

The purpose of using sub-headings is as much for the writer as it is for the reader. Sub-headings promote organization—both of thought and expression. Your choice of sub-headings should be simple and direct. Often, you need look no further than the topics identified in the interrogatory, i.e., "Motion for Summary Judgment," "Identification of Damages," "Easement by Prescription." Examples of additional sub-heading topics include parties and causes of action, i.e., "George v. ABC Company," "Breach of Contract."

2. Write on only one side of the paper

If you write on only one side of the paper in the booklet, the left side is available to add explanatory notes. Hopefully, your use of an outline will avoid the need to direct the reader to additional notes but should it become necessary, this is the least disruptive method of doing so.

3. Write in paragraph form

You would be surprised how many candidates forget the dictates of basic paragraph formation and write in a "stream of consciousness" style worthy of William Faulkner. When your essay appears as one solid mass to a grader who has but minutes to spend per paper, imagine the result. Instead, make your paper easy on the eyes. Use paragraphs to show your progression of thought and the sequence of your analysis. Indent and skip a line between paragraphs. Whatever you do to make your grader's job easier, makes you the grateful beneficiary.

4. Do not overly rely on underlining, capitalizing, etc.

If you emphasize everything you write, the effect is lost. You can underline "buzz words" but if you are writing in the language of the law, all you write is worthy of note.

L. EMERGENCY MEASURES OR "WHAT TO DO IF"

1. You freeze and begin to panic

Aside from the usual exam jitters, the bar exam does present a unique set of circumstances. After all, it's not many tests that we take with thousands of other candidates at the same time and place. The surroundings alone prove problematic for some. Assuming, however, that this is not the cause of your fright but rather, you've just read the question and your mind has gone blank. Now what do you do?

If you begin to feel panicky, stop whatever you're doing and breathe deeply. You want to regain your sense of control and composure immediately. Implement the following step-by-step approach:

(a) Review the question.

(b) Start with what you know: identify the area of law again and see if it provides insight.

(c) Focus on the basics. See if you can provide definitions. Remember, rules are really just definitions. The next step is to see if you can build on these definitions to write your paragraph of law.

(d) Finally, call on the resources you developed in law school. Lawyers act; they do not react. Think deliberately and respond accordingly.

2.   You don't know the rule of law

This is everyone's greatest fear, law student and lawyer alike. What you must do is learn to rely on your training and instinct. Force yourself to go through the following steps:

First, ask

"What is the issue?" You can formulate this from the question you are directed to answer. Even if you're not sure of the rule, you can figure out

what it is that the examiners want you to consider. Focusing on identifying the issue will allow you to regain your composure and lead you back to the structure of thinking like a lawyer.

Write the issue, whether or not you "know" the rule you need to apply. Formulating the issue will get you points from the grader because it shows that you can identify the legal problem from the facts.

Second, ask

"What principle of law is implicated by this issue?" Now you're thinking like a lawyer.

This will either lead you to the rule from the recesses of your memory or you'll have to improvise. When you improvise, rely on your knowledge of general legal principles and standards to guide you. Use what you know about the law in general to build a specific rule for your problem.

In such cases, begin by identifying the general legal concept implicated in the problem. Some possible questions to ask include,

- Has there been a violation of a fiduciary obligation?

- Are the standards of due process /equal protection implicated?

- Has the requirement of good faith been breached?

- Are the "best interests of the child" at stake?

These questions become your starting point. As you study, you'll find more basic questions that you can rely upon to trigger your thought process. Think of them as your mental checklist.

For example, if you're asked about recoverable "damages" in a particular case, rely on what you know about "damages" in particular areas of the law and proceed from there.

(a) If it's a contracts problem, you know every breach of contract entitles the aggrieved party to sue for damages. The general theory of damages in contract actions is that the injured party should be placed in the same position as if the contract had been properly performed, at least so far as money can do this. Compensatory damages are designed to give the plaintiff the "benefit of his bargain."

(b) On the other hand, if it's a torts problem, you know that the overall goal is to compensate plaintiff for harm which he or she has sustained because defendant breached a duty.

And finally, even if you can't find the issue or principle of law, you can break down the problem into the elements common to every case and proceed from there:

(a) Identify the parties and the nature of their relationship.

Is it that of employer/employee, landlord/tenant, buyer/seller, parent/child, husband/wife ?

(b) Identify the place(s) where the facts arose.

Did the events occur in a public area, a private home, a school, a waterway, a farm?

(c) Identify whether objects or things were involved.

Was there a transaction involving the sale of goods? Is the ownership of land or chattel in dispute?

(d) Identify the acts or omissions which form the basis of the action.

Was there a robbery, an assault, an act of discrimination?

(e) Determine whether there is a defense to the action.

Is there a basis for self-defense, justification, privilege?

(f) Characterize the relief sought.

Are the parties seeking damages? Are they monetary or equitable damages, or both?

These questions allow you to gain access to the problem when your initial read is fruitless. From any one of these topics, it is but a short step to finding the principle of law implicated in the question. It might be a very good idea to memorize these topics and have them readily available to "jump-start" your thought process.

M. BAR EXAMINATION ESSAY WRITING CHECKLIST

I. Allocating your Time

1. Do you have your watch somewhere in plain view?

2.   Did you set up a timetable on your scrap paper?

II.   Reading the Question

1.   Did you begin by reading the interrogatory at the end of the question?

2.   If you're asked to evaluate court rulings, have you located these rulings in the fact pattern?

3.   Did you read the fact pattern "actively"?

   a) Have you identified the area of law and the legal relationship between the parties?

   b) Have you circled amounts of money, dates, locations, quantities, and ages?

   c) Have you noted the words "oral" and "written"?

   d) Are you perfectly clear about *who is doing what to whom*?

III.   Outlining your Answer

1.   Have you used the interrogatories in the essay to determine the number of issues you need to identify?

2.   Have you used the number of issues to set up the numbering scheme for your outline?

3.   Have you articulated an issue for each interrogatory?

4.   For each issue, have you compiled the building blocks for the rule of law by considering,

    a) elements?

    b) definitions?

    c) exceptions to the general rule?

    d) distinctions?

5.   Have you followed a hierarchy of concepts by,

    a) moving from the general to the specific?

    b) defining each legal term of art?

IV.   *Writing the Essay*

1.   Does your statement of the issue begin with, **"The issue is whether"**? and include the word **"when"** to ensure that you include the relevant facts?

2.   Does your statement of the rule commence with, **"Under the** [state the controlling law: common law, federal rule, state-specific statute, etc.]?

3.   Did you use **"Here"** or **"In this case"** to introduce your application?

4.   Did you use **"because"** to make the connection between rule and fact?

5.   Does your statement of the conclusion begin with **"Therefore"**?

6.   Did you match up a "fact" with each "element" or "definition" in your rule of law?

7.   Have you answered the question you were asked?

CHAPTER 6

THE MULTISTATE QUESTIONS

A. ABOUT THE MBE

Multiple choice questions: You either love 'em or hate 'em. No one is ever neutral about them. And with good reason. Your answer is either right or wrong. There's no middle ground or opportunity for partial credit. On an essay, you can score some points even when you've taken a wrong turn if you provide a thoughtful and well-reasoned analysis of the issues and legal principles involved. No such luck with a multiple choice question.

Regardless of how you feel about multiple choice questions, however, you have to deal with 200 of them on the Multistate portion of the bar exam. And unless you're planning to move to Louisiana or Washington, you can't escape them: as of February, 2003, the MBE is administered in 48 states and the District of Columbia.

1. When it's Given

The MBE is given twice a year in most jurisdictions: on the last Wednesday in February and on the last Wednesday in July. The state-specific portion of the bar exam is given either the day(s) before or the day(s) after the MBE. There are a few states that offer the MBE only once a year so as I've said before, it's your job to consult your individual jurisdiction for precise information. A regularly updated list of each jurisdiction's bar admission office address and phone number can be found at *www. ncbex.org*.

2.   What it's Like

The MBE is an objective six-hour examination, consisting of 200 multiple choice questions. It's divided into two periods of three hours each: one in the morning and one in the afternoon, each containing 100 questions. Applicants are asked to choose the *best* answer from four alternatives. Since your score is based on the number of correctly answered questions, you're advised to answer every question. Even if you have no idea as to the correct answer, it's still appropriate to guess because you're not penalized for incorrect answers.

Each jurisdiction sets its own policy with respect to the relative weight given to the MBE score. Consequently, if you have any questions with respect to the use made of your MBE score in calculating your overall bar passage score, you must direct such inquiries to your individual jurisdiction and not the National Conference of Bar Examiners.

3.   What Subjects are Tested

Multiple choice questions are used because they allow the examiners to test a wide range of topics. The MBE covers six subjects: Constitutional Law, Contracts, Criminal Law, Evidence, Real Property, and Torts. The questions are presented in a completely random manner so that both the subject matter and the complexity of the question varies from one question to the next. This means that you might go from a Contracts question to a Property question and on to an Evidence question. You'll also have to figure out the subject for yourself since you're not told which area is being tested for any question. Once again, your ability to read "actively" is essential.

As of July, 1997, there are 34 questions each on Contracts and Torts and 33 questions each on Constitutional Law, Criminal Law, Evidence, and Real Property. Out of the 34 Contracts questions, approximately 25% of the questions are based on provisions of the Uniform Commercial Code, Articles 1 and 2. Out of the 33 Criminal Law questions, approximately 40% of the questions are based on Criminal Procedure issues arising under the 4th, 5th and 6th Amendments.

The Bar Examiners provide some guidance in helping you narrow the fields in these subjects. In its Information Booklet to bar candidates, the NCBE provides individual subject matter outlines for the six subject areas. Each subject matter outline indicates the scope of coverage for that particular subject. You're also given a breakdown by percentage of just how many questions will be taken from a particular category. While you're still responsible for knowing what amounts to a prodigious amount of law, the outlines make it manageable by narrowing the range of each subject and delineating the precise topics. If you use these outlines appropriately during your preparation, you can target and focus your energies where it will do the most good.

4.   Why it's Challenging

The MBE poses a challenge for even the best students. It's a challenge because there are so many questions and so little time. It's a challenge because it tests your knowledge of the substantive law, your reading comprehension and reasoning skills, your ability to work quickly and efficiently, and your capacity to remain focused and functioning over a long period of time.

So what's a candidate to do? You need to prepare properly by recognizing the specific skills that are tested on the MBE and then fine-tuning those skills. The MBE tests two abilities: mastery of the substantive law and the ability to analyze a question. Your bar review course provides you with all the substantive law you need to know; your law school education has taught you how "to think like a lawyer." MBE questions require that you put the two together in a very special way.

B.   STUDYING FOR THE MBE

Studying for the MBE, a short-answer, objective exam, is not the same as studying for other types of exams. It requires not only that you memorize the rules of law but that you fully understand them. If you don't know the rules with precision and specificity and truly comprehend how they fit together, you won't be able to find the issue in the facts, apply the rule, and select the best answer from among the four answer choices in the span of the 1.8 seconds you have for each question. Simply memorizing rules from flash cards and outlines won't guarantee that you'll recognize them when they're tested in a fact pattern. Instead, you must learn the rules in the context in which they're likely to appear.

Such an understanding of the law usually comes only with real experience–but in the fictionalized world of the MBE, even real life wouldn't prepare you adequately for the way that the bar examiners like to test the rules, the elements of rules, and the exceptions to the rules. In this case, the only meaningful way to prepare for the MBE is to practice from actual MBE questions. Anything else is, as they say, "close, but no cigar."

1. Working with the "Real Thing"

Fortunately, the NCBE knows this is the most effective way to prepare for the MBE and offers candidates the opportunity to purchase past exams. The Information Booklet contains an MBE Study Aids Order Form and makes previously published MBE questions available to you for purchase. The order form is also available on the Bar Examiners' web site. Periodically, as old MBE questions are retired, the bar examiners release them and make them available to you. Such questions are a treasure trove to the candidate preparing for the bar exam.

If you're like most candidates, however, you're probably thinking that the last thing you need are more "study aids." On the contrary: these are not study aids but insights into the minds of the Bar Examiners. Besides, after spending upwards of $80,000 on a legal education, now is not the time to be frugal about an additional $50 or so. Since the Bar Examiners write and evaluate and score the questions, doesn't it just make sense to spend your time getting to know how they frame the questions and what they consider the best answer?

2.   Learning the Details and Nuances

As you can see from the subject outlines, the scope of subject coverage on the MBE is very broad. This means that the questions are spread out over a variety of topics and are not "lumped" in any particular area. Even though it may seem that the topic you dread most is showing up on every other question, this is simply not the case.

The breadth of subject coverage is only one consideration when you study for the MBE: you must also consider that the MBE is a national exam. In answering questions, you're responsible for knowing and applying the *majority rule* and not that of your local jurisdiction. All too many bar candidates forget that the MBE tests the current prevailing view and instead apply the local rule of the jurisdiction to answer the MBE question. To avoid this problem and not be distracted by your knowledge of minority views and local rules, you must wear "blinders" on MBE day.

Practicing the questions is no substitute for knowing the black letter law. And know it you must to answer the questions. A superficial understanding of broad concepts won't be enough to allow you to distinguish between the answer choices. You need a detailed understanding of the rules. As you'll see from the following example, the MBE tests details, not generalities:

On December 15, Lawyer received from Stationer, Inc., a retailer of office supplies, an offer consisting of its catalog and a signed letter stating, "We will supply you with as many of the items in the enclosed catalog as you order during the next calendar year. We assure you that this offer and the prices in the catalog will remain firm throughout the coming year."

For this question only, assume that no other correspondence passed between Stationer and Lawyer until the following April 15 (four months later), when Stationer received from Lawyer a faxed order for "100 reams of your paper, catalog item #101."

Did Lawyer's April 15 fax constitute an effective acceptance of Stationer's offer at the prices specified in the catalog?

(A) Yes, because Stationer had not revoked its offer before April 15.

(B) Yes, because a one-year option contract had been created by Stationer's offer.

(C) No, because under applicable law the irrevocability of Stationer's offer was limited to a period of three months.

(D) No, because Lawyer did not accept Stationer's offer within a reasonable time.

Here the Bar Examiners are looking to trap those candidates with only a superficial knowledge of the contract rules regarding acceptance and the Uniform Commercial Code's rule regarding "firm offers."

Answer Choice (A) is the best answer because it correctly applies the rules regarding the revocability of an offer to the facts of this problem. A candidate can be easily misled in this question by confusing the UCC's "firm offer," the common law's "option contract," and the general principles regarding the revocability of offers.

Analysis begins with articulation of the issue in the fact pattern. The question is whether and on what basis Stationer's offer was still capable of acceptance on April 15. Because this is a transaction involving the sale of goods from a merchant (Stationer is a "retailer of office supplies" so he is "merchant" within the meaning of Article 2), the offer made in the signed writing of December 15 constituted a "firm offer."

Now you need to summon the rule of law: a firm offer is "an offer by a merchant to buy or sell goods in a signed writing (''record'' in Revised UCC) which by its terms gives assurance that it will be held open [and] is not revocable, for lack of consideration, during the time stated or if no time is stated for a reasonable time, but in no event may such period of irrevocability exceed three months. . . .'' UCC 2–205.

Answer Choice (C) is clearly the bar examiner's choice to catch the unwary candidate who reacts to familiar language and misreads the significance of words in the fact pattern. Here the answer choice states that the applicable rule would limit the irrevocability of the offer to a period of three months and the fact pattern makes it a specific point to observe that four months had passed. While Answer Choice (C) states the rule of law correctly, and it is true that four months have passed since the making of the offer, this does not mean that the offer is automatically revoked. The rule serves only to prohibit the merchant from revoking during this time: it need not be revoked. After the three months, the merchant may choose to revoke the offer or not. Since the offer was not revoked after the three month period when the merchant could have revoked the ''firm offer,'' then Lawyer was capable of acceptance, as the rationale in Choice (A) provides.

3. You Must Be Prepared

As this one example demonstrates quite nicely, you must prepare for the MBE by mastering the black letter law with a level of detailed sophistication. The bar exam is meant to weed out those with anything less. This is not to say, however, that you must walk into the bar exam expecting to know every single rule of law and its fine distinctions. Even if you had all the time in the world to prepare and the memory of an elephant, this wouldn't be possible or necessary to pass the exam. You're not aiming for an "A" or to be at the top of your class. You just want to pass!

4.   How to Prepare

Your preparation for the MBE therefore requires that you combine your knowledge of the theoretical with the practical. Your goal is twofold: to acquire a detailed understanding of the substantive law and master the specific manner in which it is tested. In order to acquire this type of knowledge, you need to prepare by practicing the rules in the context in which they are tested. For example, after you've completed a bar review class on an area of the law and reviewed your notes, you're ready to go to work on answering multiple choice questions.

5.   What Does It Mean to "Do" Multistate Questions?

Suppose you were to sit at your desk and answer as many Multistate questions as you could in 60 minutes. At the end of the hour, you'd check your answers and tally your score. Then you'd go on and "do" another set of questions, once again tallying the number of correct responses at the end of the session. Assuming you've put in a couple of hours and "done" about 65 questions or so, you'd call it a day. You'd pack up your books and commend yourself for studying for the MBE. But did you?

Let's say you answered half of the questions correctly.

- Does this mean that you "know" 50% of the material?

- Can you be sure your correct responses were "correct" for the right reasons?

- Do you know why your incorrect responses were wrong?

- Did you select an incorrect answer choice because you didn't know or failed to identify the controlling rule of law?

- Did you identify the correct rule but apply it incorrectly to the facts?

- Did you misread the call-of-the-question?

- Did you misread the facts?

Unless you can answer these questions, the hours you've just spent "doing" questions was pretty much a waste of time. Regrettably, too many candidates believe that this way of "doing" Multistate questions will lead to a passing Multistate score. Typically, it doesn't. This approach doesn't work because while you may have "answered" questions, you've not learned to "analyze" questions. And you must know how to reason through a question to arrive at the correct answer choice. Not only is this process essential to arriving at the correct answer, but you must be conscious of how you've reasoned through a problem so that you can go back and examine that thought process should you make an incorrect choice.

6. "Doing" it Right

Let's start over. You attended your bar review class where the topic was contract formation. After class, you reviewed your notes and otherwise "studied" contract formation. You're convinced that you pretty much know all there is to know about the topics of offer and acceptance. Now you're ready to work on Multistate questions and here's how you're going to do it:

a. Select a group of MBE questions from the specific area of law you've just reviewed.

In this case, you're going to answer only questions dealing with contract formation issues.

Note: *When you order sample MBE questions from the Bar Examiners, you're sent an actual 200–item exam. Therefore, you'll have to peruse the questions first to identify those which pertain to your topic. Simply make a list of those question numbers on your answer sheet and follow the list when answering the questions.*

By practicing groups of questions in a particular area of the law, you can:

- Identify your strengths and weaknesses.

  If you consistently answer questions dealing with a particular rule of law incorrectly, this means that you need to return to your notes and review that topic more thoroughly before attempting more MBE questions.

- Begin to see patterns in the facts.

  When you practice questions of a particular type together, you can see their common characteristics and realize that there are only so many variations of a fact pattern with respect to a single legal issue. This allows you to become familiar with the way particular topics are tested. As a result, your comfort level increases.

- Become familiar with the Bar Examiners' specific use of language.

  In addition to becoming familiar with the types of facts that invoke certain rules, by working with groups of questions in a particular area, you also become accustomed to the Bar Examiners' very specific use of vocabulary. Very often, the difference between a correct and incorrect answer choice turns on the meaning and significance attached to particular language in the fact pattern. Your ability to identify such words is critical and only practice with actual MBE questions will provide the opportunity to gain this familiarity.

Here's an example from a past MBE that shows how attuned you must be to the signals in the language as well as the rules:

Structo contracted with Bailey to construct for $500,000 a warehouse and an access driveway at a highway level. Shortly after commencing work on the driveway, which required for the specified level some excavation and removal of surface material, Structo unexpectedly encountered a large mass of solid rock.

For this question only, assume the following facts. Structo informed Bailey (accurately) that because of the rock the driveway as specified would cost at least $20,000 more than figured, and demanded for that reason a total contract price of $520,000. Since Bailey was expecting warehousing customers immediately after the agreed completion date, he signed a writing promising to pay the additional $20,000. Following timely completion of the warehouse and driveway, which conformed to the contract in all respects, Bailey refused to pay Structo more than $500,000.

What is the maximum amount to which Structo is entitled?

(A) $500,000, because there was no consideration for Bailey's promise to pay the additional $20,000.

(B) $500,000, because Bailey's promise to pay the additional $20,000 was exacted under duress.

(C) $520,000, because the modification was fair and was made in the light of circumstances not anticipated by the parties when the original contract was made.

(D) $520,000, provided that the reasonable value of Structo's total performance was that much or more.

Here, your ability to select the correct answer choice depends on whether you attach the appropri-

ate legal significance to two words that appear in
the fact pattern: "unexpectedly" and "accurately."
If you read quickly, instead of actively, it's very easy
to miss these signal words. But if you do, you'll
overlook legally relevant facts: first, that finding a
solid mass of rock was *unanticipated* ("unexpected"); and second, that Structo was acting in *good
faith* ("accurately") when he told Bailey that the
cost of putting in the driveway would cost more
than originally contemplated.

Unless you draw the appropriate inferences from
these words, you won't conclude that the parties
entered into a valid modification when Structo
asked for more money to complete the job which
required more work than originally bargained for by
the parties and Bailey signed a writing promising to
pay the additional $20,000. Instead, you'll find a
lack of consideration (Answer Choice A), be led
down the path of coercion (Answer Choice B), or
possibly allow a recovery in restitution (Answer
Choice D). Sadly, each incorrect answer choice
would be for "want of a word."

While time is indeed a pressing factor, you can
see that it's more important to read actively than it
is to read quickly. Fortunately, it's far easier to
become an active reader than it is to become a
faster reader. It just takes practice.

   *b. Answer a question and immediately check
your response*

By verifying your answer choice right after you've
selected it, the fact pattern is still fresh in your

mind and, hopefully, so is your reasoning for select-ing that answer. Getting immediate feedback on your analysis of the question serves two functions: first, it reinforces your understanding of the rule if your answer choice was correct; and second, it al-lows you to assess quickly the flaw in your analysis if your answer choice was incorrect.

(1) *If you answered correctly:*

Read the explanation for the correct answer choice if explanations are available. Even if you answered correctly, you want to make sure that you did so for the right reason. Many a candidate will get an answer "correct" for an "incorrect" reason and therefore can't rely on really "knowing" the material. In this case, if you got the "right" answer for the "wrong" reason, proceed as if you answered incorrectly.

(2) *If you answered incorrectly:*

If you made an incorrect answer choice, then you must go back to the question, reread it, and before you try to answer again, ask yourself the following questions:

- What is the legal problem presented by the facts?
- What rule do I apply to address the problem?
- What do I think should be the outcome?
- Which of the answer choices state this out-come?

If these questions don't lead you to choose the correct response, then you must return to your notes and review that particular topic in depth until you can.

Similarly, if you don't fully appreciate the explanation offered for the correct answer choice or can't provide one of your own, then you must return to your study materials and review the law until you can do so. These are the only ways to ensure that you fully comprehend a topic.

c.   The Timing Factor

To time or not to time? That is so often the question. Bar candidates frequently ask me whether they should time themselves when they practice their MBE questions. My answer is the one they always appreciate: "it depends."

Think about it: does an athlete set world records during practice or during the competition? Clearly, then, how quickly you can "race" through the questions during your practice sessions is of no particular value. What matters is what you learn when you practice and how you ultimately perform on bar day.

During practice, you're concentrating on learning the black letter law, how the Bar Examiners test that law, and the language they use to phrase the questions. If this is your goal when you practice Multistate questions (or any part of the exam), then how long it takes you to read and answer the questions is not the issue. Rather, it's whether you absorbed anything meaningful from the practice. It doesn't matter how long it takes you to answer a question, but whether you answered the question correctly and did so for the correct reason. I can practically guarantee that once you become comfortable with the process of analyzing the questions, your speed in answering them will automatically increase.

Still, I strongly recommend that you plan for a minimum of two or three "timed" sessions when preparing for the MBE. A couple of sessions should be devoted to determining whether you can meet the general guideline of answering 17 questions in a 30–minute period. You must average 33–34 questions per hour to complete the 100 questions in the three-hour MBE sessions.

Further, at least one practice session should be a simulation of a complete three-hour test period covering 100 questions. You need to know whether you can sustain your concentration for such a long period of time. It's a very different experience to answer 100 questions than it is to answer 25 questions. It's also a different experience when the questions come at you in a completely random manner as opposed to the topical approach you've been following during your practice sessions where you know the general subject matter of the questions. Unless you've had an opportunity to perform under these conditions, you won't be able to assess your performance accurately.

You'll be surprised at what you might learn about yourself from a three-hour session. For example, you might find that you don't get into the swing of things until question number 15 or so. This means that you're in danger of losing valuable points up front simply because you need to "warm up." If you learn this about yourself during practice, you can compensate on bar day by doing what I've had some of my students do: get up 30 minutes earlier than planned and answer a round of questions *before* heading into the exam. By getting 15 questions "under your belt" before the exam begins, you're warmed up and ready to go at test time.

Similarly, you may find that you lose momentum in the middle or towards the end of the test period. If you find it difficult to sustain your concentration, lose your focus, or find yourself rereading passages because you can't remember what you've just read, then you're most likely in need of an energy boost. During practice, you should experiment with various snacks to see which supply the energy you need. Remember, if you're a caffeine addict, you won't be able to get a cup of coffee during the exam, so you need to explore the alternatives. Some students have told me that chocolate covered espresso beans work wonders. Others have found energy bars fit the bill. Your job during these practice sessions is to find what works for you.

d.   *"Skipping About" on the exam*

In addition to issues of timing, candidates often ask whether they should "skip around" when answering questions on the MBE. Some believe that the first twenty questions and the last twenty questions are "easier" and therefore, they should answer those first and then go back to the others. As I've indicated earlier, MBE questions appear in completely random order, both in terms of subject matter and complexity. Consequently, there is no benefit to be derived from jumping around but quite possibly there is a detriment: you can lose your place on the answer sheet and enter your selections incorrectly. Also, it takes time to read a question, decide to skip it, and then return to read it again later. You simply don't have this extra time. However, if you find that you must skip some questions to return later, then be careful to mark your answer sheet appropriately when you return.

Finally, remember that you've had some meaningful experience in this area; you're not a complete novice when it comes to taking exams. You've taken exams throughout your law school career. Use this experience to guide you now.

C. STRATEGIES FOR MASTERING THE MBE

While this section may be titled "Strategies for Mastering the MBE," the truth is that there are no tricks to be learned, only the law. If there is a strategy, it's to be prepared through practice and knowledge. As a result, the following techniques will show you how to analyze MBE questions and become so familiar with their structure and content that on bar day, you'll work through the questions efficiently and accurately.

The strategies are divided into two sections: those that provide general guidelines to approaching the questions and those that are targeted to specific topics. As you'll see, most of the guidelines amount to little more than common sense approaches based on logic and knowledge of the material to be tested.

1.   General Guidelines

a.   *Be familiar with the structure of MBE questions*

As you've no doubt already noticed, MBE questions adhere to a particular structure. There is the factual situation followed by the interrogatory or "call-of-the question." While most questions will follow this format, in some cases you'll have one fact setting and a series of questions based on those facts. Typically, each of the questions will provide additional facts or change the facts in some way so you must be sure to read each question as if it were a new question entirely.

b.   *Read actively*

Just as you've learned to read essay fact patterns "actively," you must do so with MBE questions. Because of time constraints, you'll have time for only one reading of the fact pattern. However, don't make the mistake of sacrificing a careful reading for a quick one. You must read carefully to spot signal words and legally significant facts. The following are some points you should look for as you read:

- Relationships between parties that signal the area of law and legal duties: landlord/tenant, employer/employee, principal/agent, buyer/seller.

- Amounts of money, dates, quantities, and ages.

- Words such as "oral" and "written", "reasonable" and "unreasonable", among others.

- Words which indicate the actor's state of mind such as "intended", "decided", "mistakenly thought", and "deliberately", among others.

Since you may write in the test booklet, circle or highlight these words and others which "legally" characterize the behavior of the actors.

c. Never "assume" facts

The Bar Examiners carefully construct MBE questions to contain all the facts you need to answer the question. You must rely solely on these facts, and no others, to answer the question. Of course you may draw reasonable inferences from the facts but you cannot fabricate your own or create "what if" scenarios. Unfortunately, too many bar candidates allow their creative side to surface when reading these questions and stray from the fact pattern.

In addition to keeping to the facts, don't let yourself go off on tangents based on possible theories you see raised in the facts. Sometimes when you read a fact pattern, you'll see the potential for a number of possible causes of action. In such instances, you must refrain from anticipating what the Bar Examiners will ask by moving forward on your own and formulating responses based on what you "think" might be asked. This is one of the very reasons you'll read the question stem before you read the fact pattern—to keep you from going astray. Potentially, this is just as dangerous as misreading or adding facts. Not only does it lead to possible incorrect answer choices but it needlessly saps your time and mental energy.

d. Avoid temptation and stick to the law

Just as you must remain focused on the facts as presented in the question, you must apply the rule of law to the facts without hesitation or equivocation. You cannot get emotionally involved with the parties or substitute your instincts for what you know is legally correct. It's not your place to find a criminal defendant not guilty when in fact his actions satisfied every element of the crime according to the statute. Or vice versa: if an act does not violate the provisions of a given statute, then whatever you happen to think about the nature of the act (or actor) doesn't matter. It's not a crime if the jurisdiction doesn't make it one. I cannot say it often enough: your job is to follow the law and apply it to the facts mechanically.

Similarly, the bar exam is not the time or place to become "practical" and consider what you think would happen in actual practice. Many candidates have defended their incorrect answer choices to me by explaining "I know it couldn't happen like that in practice. That's why I didn't choose that answer." My response is that this isn't "real" life. It's the bar exam! This is not to say, however, that bar exam questions have nothing to do with the practice of law or the "real rules." It's just that on the bar exam, as in law school, we are studying and working with the theoretical rule of law and what should be, not necessarily what is. The bar exam is no time to worry about the great divide between theory and practice—simply apply the rule of law as you've learned it to answer the questions and you'll be fine.

2.   Tactics for Analyzing the Questions

The following are the five basic steps to follow in answering each and every MBE question. After a bit of practice, this process will become second nature to you, but I admit that in the beginning it will seem artificial, almost contrived, to approach a question this way. But you'll soon see that it yields results.

For each question, you will:

- Act and not react.

- Read actively from the bottom up.

- Find the issue.

- Move from the issue to articulation of your own answer.

- Translate your "answer" to fit an available "answer choice."

a. *Act, do not react*

Perhaps because of the stringent time constraints on the MBE, the tendency to panic is greatest on this section of the bar exam. But when you panic, you're no longer in control. When you give up control, you're at the mercy of the answer choices. Then they pick you, instead of the other way around. I'm not going to let you fall into this trap. Instead, each time you answer an MBE question, you're going to "act" in response to the question presented and not "react" to the answer choices.

How do you act and not react to the answer choices? *Simple: you have an answer in mind before you even look at the answer choices.*

b. *Read actively from the bottom up*

Begin each MBE question by reading the question stem. Reading the interrogatory first serves two important functions:

- First, it helps to identify the area of law. Often, but not always, you can determine the subject area of the problem from the call-of-the-question. Then you can use this information to inform your subsequent reading of the fact pattern.

- Second, it often identifies the point of view you must adopt to answer the question. For example, if you're asked to determine a party's most likely claim or best defense, then you'll want to read the fact pattern with an emphasis on that party's point of view.

After reading the interrogatory, you're ready to read the fact pattern. After reading the hypo and the question stem once again, you're ready to conceive of an answer.

c.   Find the issue

Your ability to identify the main issue in each question will be crucial to selecting the correct answer choice. For most candidates, it's not intuitive to engage in an IRAC analysis to answer an objective multiple choice question. However, MBE questions are organized around a central issue in the fact pattern and individual issues in each of the responses. The only way to distinguish between the answer choices is to identify the legal question raised in the fact pattern.

The process is the same you use to spot issues in essay questions. In fact, it's most like the steps you take to identify the issues in essays following the New York model. Your task after you've read the interrogatory is to ask yourself: *"What is the legal theory behind this question?* As soon as you've identified the legal theory, you're in a position to articulate the rule of law that addresses that issue.

Consider the following example from a past MBE:

Penstock owned a large tract of land on the shore of a lake. Drury lived on a stream that ran along one boundary of Penstock's land and into the lake. At some time in the past, a channel had been cut across Penstock's land from the stream to the lake at a point some distance from the mouth of the stream. From where Drury lived, the channel served as a convenient shortcut to the lake. Erroneously believing that the channel was a public waterway, Drury made frequent trips through the channel in his motorboat. His use of the channel caused no harm to the land through which it passed.

(A) Judgment for Penstock for nominal damages, because Drury intentionally used the channel.

(B) Judgment for Drury, if he did not use the channel after learning of Penstock's ownership claim.

(C) Judgment for Drury, because he caused no harm to Penstock's land.

(D) Judgment for Drury, because when he used the channel he believed it was a public waterway.

In this question, once you've identified the issue in the fact pattern, the correct answer will practically pick you. But you must be very specific and narrow in your articulation of the issue in order to differentiate between the answer choices.

Here, the issue is whether Drury trespassed on Pennstock's property even though he "erroneously believed" it was a public waterway and he caused "no harm to the land." Once you articulate this issue, and summon the rule of trespass, it is a quick move to the correct answer choice, which is Choice (A).

d. *Move from issue to answer*

After you've identified the issue raised in the facts, apply the rule of law to the facts, and reach a conclusion—all without so much as a peek at the answer choices. By determining the appropriate outcome before looking at the answer choices, you're in control and not at the mercy of the Bar Examiners' distractors.

You must move carefully from articulation of the issue to your "answer" and from your "answer" to identifying the correct "answer choice."

e. *Fill the gap from "answer" to "answer choice"*

After you've decided what the answer should be, you're ready to look at the answer choices. Don't expect the Bar Examiners to phrase the answer in precisely the words you're looking for—these words won't be there. Instead, you'll have to "fill the gap" between your words and the words the Bar Examiners have chosen to express the answer. And the Bar Examiners do such a good job of camouflage that candidates often don't recognize the correct response even though it "says" exactly what they want!

Consider the following MBE question, where the array of answer choices nicely illustrates the dangers that await the unwary candidate:

Hydro–King, Inc. a high-volume, pleasure-boat retailer, entered into a written contract with Boater, signed by both parties, to sell Boater a power boat for $12,000. The manufacturer's price of the boat delivered to Hydro–King was $9,500. As the contract provided, Boater paid Hydro–King $4,000 in advance and promised to pay the full balance upon delivery of the boat. The contract contained no provision for liquidated damages. Prior to the agreed delivery date, Boater notified Hydro–King that he would be financially unable to conclude the purchase; and Hydro–King thereupon resold the same boat that Boater had ordered to a third person for $12,000 cash.

If Boater sues Hydro–King for restitution of the $4,000 advance payment, which of the following should the court decide?

(A) Boater's claim should be denied, because, as the party in default, he is deemed to have lost any right to restitution of a benefit conferred on Hydro–King.

(B) Boater's claim should be denied, because, but for his repudiation, Hydro–King would have made a profit on two boat sales instead of one.

(C) Boater's claim should be upheld in the amount of $4,000 minus the amount of Hydro–King's lost profit under its contract with Boater.

(D) Boater's claims should be upheld in the amount of $3,500 ($4,000 minus $500 as statutory damages under the UCC).

In this question, the issue is what, if anything, is a buyer entitled to when the buyer repudiates a sale and the seller re-sells the item but would have sold it to the second buyer anyway? It's the classic case of the lost volume seller. Application of the rule tells us that the seller is entitled to receive his lost profit on the first deal—the one he made with the repudiating seller. Under these facts, that would be $2,500 (the sales price of $12,000 minus the manufacturer's cost of $9,500). So Hydro–King would have made a $2,500 profit from Boater and is entitled to keep $2,500 of the $4,000 advance payment and Boater gets back $1,500.

Now I'm ready to find this answer among the answer choices. Of course, it's not going to appear in precisely these words. Instead, I'll have to determine which of the answer choices leads to the same result. Answer Choice (C), the correct answer, effectively states the result I've reached. Boater's claim is $4,000—less Hydro–King's lost profit. Answer Choice (B) is not completely correct because while it acknowledges Hydro–King's entitlement to its profit on both sales, it requires that Boater's claim be denied in its entirety. As we know, this need not be the case where, as here, the advance payment was in excess of the lost profit.

3. Tactics for Analyzing the Answers

a. *Identify the issue in each answer choice*

Not only is there an "issue" in the fact pattern, but there is an "issue" in each answer choice.

Actually, it's more of a legal theory that's operating in each of the answer choices and unless you figure out the individual theories, you won't be able to distinguish between the answer choices.

Let's see how this works with an actual MBE. In fact, we can return to one we've already examined and look solely at the answer choices. Remember our friends Structo and Bailey and the large mass of solid rock that appeared after excavation for the driveway had begun? Here we need to look at the theories operating in each of the answer choices.

- (A) $500,000, because there was no consideration for Bailey's promise to pay the additional $20,000.

- (B) $500,000, because Bailey's promise to pay the additional $20,000 was exacted under duress.

- (C) $520,000, because the modification was fair and was made in the light of circumstances not anticipated by the parties when the original contract was made.

- (D) $520,000, provided that the reasonable value of Structo's total performance was that much or more.

Answer Choice (A) raises the question of whether there was a bargained-for exchange for Bailey's promise to pay the additional $20,000. You need to determine whether Structo's promise to do more work than originally bargained for in excavating the driveway was consideration. And it was, so Choice A is not the answer.

Answer Choice (B) requires that you know a case of economic duress when you see one. The issue is whether Bailey was unfairly coerced into modifying the agreement. The facts do state that Bailey was expecting warehouse customers immediately after the completion date of the project but they also state that Structo "accurately" informed Bailey that the presence of the rock made the job more expensive than anticipated. Hence Structo was not making a wrongful threat but informing Bailey that the job would cost more. Bailey was free to consider other contractors.

The issue in Answer Choice (C) was whether the parties entered into a valid modification for the payment of $20,000 when Structo had to do more work in excavating the driveway and Bailey signed a writing promising to pay the additional $20,000. The answer choice reads like the rule of law itself.

Answer Choice (D) raises the question of whether Structo's recovery should be based on a theory of *quantum meruit*. This is a restitutionary theory of recovery but not a necessary one when the parties in fact had an enforceable contract.

As you can see, identifying the legal theory behind each answer choice enables you to distinguish between them and make an appropriate selection.

   b.   Rely on your friend "the process of elimination"

Sometimes, despite all your best efforts to work through a question according to the process outlined here, you may find that the only way to arrive at an answer choice is through the process of elimination. As we discussed earlier in this section, the Bar Examiners are particularly adept at "hiding the ball" by expressing the correct answer in a way that's less than obvious.

In these cases, you'll have to examine each of the answer choices and eliminate those that can't possibly be correct. You've already learned how to eliminate an incorrect answer choice based on whether its legal theory addresses the issue in the fact pattern. Now you'll learn some other common devices for eliminating incorrect answer choices. Even though you may be using techniques to answer the questions, you're still "acting" and not merely "reacting" to whatever sounds feasible.

When can't an answer choice be correct?

(1) When it's not completely correct.

The first rule for eliminating incorrect answer choices is that an answer choice must be entirely correct or it is wrong. Suppose, for example, that an answer choice recites a correct statement of the rule of law but its application to the facts in the problem is flawed. Or vice versa: perhaps the answer choice is factually correct but cites an inapplicable rule. In each case, the answer choice is incorrect and must be eliminated. Don't be misled simply because the statement is partially correct.

(2) When it misstates or misapplies a rule of law.

Here's where solid preparation on learning the black letter law really comes in handy. You need to know the law to distinguish between answer choices that misstate or misapply the law.

Some common examples of such errors include the following:

- Answer choices that improperly identify the requisite elements of a crime or tort by either overstating or understating the necessary elements. For example, let's return once again to our friends Peavey and Dorwin where Peavey asserts a claim in battery against Dorwin and we're looking for Dorwin's best defense. Two of the answer choices include:

  A. Dorwin did not understand that his act was wrongful.

  B. Dorwin did not desire to cause harm to Peavey.

Both Answer Choices (A) and (B) are incorrect and can be eliminated because each offers a "misstatement" of the intent element of battery. While a battery is defined as the intentional, harmful or offensive touching of another, the actor need not understand his act to be wrongful nor must he desire to cause harm to satisfy the intent element.

- Answer choices that rely on inapplicable principles of law. For example, since the MBE has adopted Article 2 of the Uniform Commercial Code, you must be sure to apply its principles to questions involving transactions in goods. If you apply a common law rule to resolve the issue, you'll reach the wrong conclusion and you can be sure it's one of the answer choices purposely included to distract you. For instance, where the common law and the UCC diverge on such points as the requirements for modifications, option contracts, and acceptances, the Bar Examiners find fertile grounds for test questions.

Of course, this is not limited to the law of contracts. The Bar Examiners make fine use of the distinctions between the Federal Rules of Evidence, the common law, and the rules of individual jurisdictions. This means that you must remain alert and apply the appropriate rule to arrive at the correct answer choice.

- Answer choices that rely on the minority rule instead of the majority rule.

The rule to be applied on the MBE is the majority rule, not the minority. It no longer matters what your Contracts or Torts professor argued "should" be the prevailing view; what counts on the MBE is the modern, prevailing view. Learn it and apply it unless directed otherwise.

(3) When it mischaracterizes the facts.

Once again, active reading skills will go far in detecting this type of error. Look for contradictions between the facts in the fact pattern and the facts as characterized in the answer choice. Such an answer choice cannot be correct. Nor can an answer choice that requires you to make assumptions that go beyond the facts in the fact pattern. While it's often necessary to make reasonable inferences, you should never have to add facts to arrive at the correct answer choice. If the Bar Examiners want you to consider additional or different facts, they will provide them.

c. Watch for "because," "if," and "unless"

Just when you thought it safe to answer a question, leave it to the Bar Examiners to muddy the waters with a single word. You'd think it would be enough to have four answer choices to test a candidate's ability to work through the details without resorting to further modification of the text of each alternative. But the Bar Examiners are experts at getting the most out of a question. With a single, well-placed word such as "because," "if," or "unless," they're able to transform the entire meaning of a sentence—and unless you're careful, your score!

While doable, dealing with "because," "if," and "unless" takes a bit of practice. It also takes active and careful reading. But you're used to the drill by now, so sharpen your pencil and get ready to circle the modifier in the answer choice.

A "modifier"—whether it's "because," "if," "unless," or some equivalent—is used in the answer choice to connect the "conclusion" (the outcome to the interrogatory) with the "reasoning" in support of that conclusion. For example, an answer choice might state,

"Yes, because Sam was a third-party beneficiary of the original Adams–Dawes agreement."

Here, "yes" is the "conclusion" or direct answer to the question asked; "Sam was a third-party beneficiary" is the reason that supports the conclusion; and "because" is the link between the two.

(1) Working with "because":

On the MBE, "because" is the predominant modifier and the simplest to master. The following is a typical "because" answer choice:

"Succeed, because Ohner had promised him that the offer would remain open until June 1."

Such "because" statements are relatively straightforward. Simply ensure that the reasoning supports the conclusion both on a factual and legal basis. If either is incorrect, then the entire answer choice is incorrect and can be eliminated.

In addition to "because," remember to look for words that act like "because" in answer choices such as "since" and "as." These words are synonyms and serve the same function as 'because." Consequently, your analysis will be the same.

(2) Working with "if":

Unlike "because," when "if" is the answer choice modifier, you need determine only whether the reasoning could support the conclusion. It need not always be true, but only possible under the facts in the hypothetical. Be alert to possible "if" synonyms: "as long as" and "so long as." Remember, "if" is a conditional word and words of condition will be the trigger in such instances.

Consider the following example from a past MBE:

Dora, who was eight years old, went to the grocery store with her mother. Dora pushed the grocery cart while her mother put items into it. Dora's mother remained near Dora at all times. Peterson, another customer in the store, noticed Dora pushing the cart in a manner that caused Peterson no concern. A short time later, the cart Dora was pushing struck Peterson in the knee, inflicting serious injury.

If Peterson brings an action, based on negligence, against Dora's mother, will Peterson prevail?

(A) Yes, if Dora was negligent.

(B) Yes, because Dora's mother is responsible for any harm caused by Dora.

(C) Yes, because Dora's mother assumed the risk of her child's actions.

(D) Yes, if Dora's mother did not adequately supervise Dora's actions.

Let's examine the "if" answer choices employing our understanding that an "if" answer need only be plausible, based on the facts, to be correct. Recall that before you get to the answer choices, you've already formulated your own possible answer based on the interrogatory. Here, since the problem is based on an action brought in negligence, your mind should be ticking off the elements of a negligence claim: duty, breach, causation, harm.

Answer Choice (A) states that Peterson will prevail in a negligence action *if* Dora was negligent. The question stem states, however, that Peterson brought the negligence action against Dora's mother, not Dora. Thus, since Answer Choice (A) doesn't directly address the question, it can't be the best answer.

On the other hand, Answer Choice (D) addresses the issue of Dora's mother's actions. It poses the situation where Dora's mother did not adequately supervise Dora. You need to ask yourself whether in this instance a finding of negligence is possible: does Dora's mother have a duty to supervise her child and would she have breached that duty if she failed to do so? In this case, she would be negligent so (D) is the correct answer choice.

(3) Working with "unless":

In its own way, "unless" is as restrictive as "because." For an "unless" answer choice to be correct, it must present the *only* circumstance under which the conclusion cannot happen. If you can conceive of even one other way the result could occur, then the answer choice cannot be correct.

Consider the following example from a past MBE.

David built in his backyard a garage that encroached two feet across the property line onto property owned by his neighbor, Prudence. Thereafter, David sold his property to Drake. Prudence was unaware, prior to David's sale to Drake, of the encroachment of the garage onto her property. When she thereafter learned of the encroachment, she sued David for damages in trespass.

In this action, will Prudence prevail?

(A)   No, unless David was aware of the encroachment when the garage was built.

(B)   No, because David no longer owns or possesses the garage.

(C)   Yes, because David knew where the garage was located, whether or not he knew where the property line was.

(D)   Yes, unless Drake was aware of the encroachment when he purchased the property.

Let's look at Choice A, the first of our two "unless" answer choices. Applying the "unless" strategy, you would ask yourself: "Is there any way Prudence could prevail if David was unaware of the encroachment when the garage was built?" Remember, as soon as you read the call of the question, you considered the definition of trespass: one who intentionally enters the land of another. All David had to do was intend to build the garage and then build it. It doesn't matter whether he was aware or unaware of the encroachment in order to commit a trespass. Consequently, Prudence could prevail and Choice A cannot be correct.

Now let's look at Choice D. This answer choice brings Drake, the subsequent purchaser of the property, into the picture. Here's a good example of eliminating an answer choice because it doesn't address the issue in the problem. Prudence has brought the trespass action against David, not Drake. Assuming, however, that you didn't see this and instead was transfixed by the "unless" modifier, you'd come to the same result but it would take longer. You'd ask, "Is there any way Prudence could prevail if Drake was unaware of the encroachment when he purchased the property?" Now you'd see that Prudence could prevail in an action against David if Drake was unaware of the encroachment. Whether Prudence has an action in trespass against Drake is simply not the issue in this question and should not be a factor in your analysis.

Choice C is the correct answer choice. The reasoning addresses the central issue in the problem which is whether David committed a trespass. What Choice C states is right on point—both legally and factually. Legally, David would have committed a trespass if he intentionally entered the land of another. The facts tell us that David built a garage that encroached on his neighbor's property. Choice C fits all the criteria and must be correct.

d. Guess, but with a strategy

While it sounds like an oxymoron to "guess with a strategy," it's true nonetheless. You've absolutely nothing to lose by guessing since there are no penalties for incorrect answers. And if you can narrow the odds only slightly, you've got a decent shot at making a correct selection.

(1) Eliminate all the obviously incorrect answer choices.

Typically, you'll find that you can safely eliminate one or even two responses as incorrect. Now that you've narrowed the field a bit, even if it's a little bit, you're ready to make the most of some informed guesses.

(2) Dismiss answer choices that address other principles or unrelated rules of law.

Of course the Bar Examiners won't be so obvious as to include evidence principles in answer choices for contracts questions, but they will include common law rules in Article 2 sales problems and cite standards for negligence when strict liability is at issue. Similarly, be alert to answer choices that seem to be from the applicable body of law but really are not. Such distractors are common in "cross-over" areas where the distinctions between subjects are blurred and somewhat artificial. For example, problems in criminal procedure may contain answer choices that draw on rules from constitutional law and evidence. Remember, it's the law school that imposes boundaries around the law for pedagogical purposes. The law itself does not impose such rigid lines.

On the other hand, do not be quick to dismiss all such cross-overs. Remember, contracts for the sale of land, while topically in property law, still require application of contract principles. And breach of warranty, while a traditional contract claim, is often asserted in products liability actions.

(3) Find your compass—the issue.

When in doubt anywhere on the bar exam—the essays, the MPT, or the MBE—remember that the legal issue is your guide. It allows you to distinguish between relevant and irrelevant rules and facts, thus providing the single most effective answer choice eliminator.

Reread the question and focus solely on finding the issue in the fact pattern. Then identify the issue addressed in each of the answer choices. One should address the issue in the fact pattern.

(4) Consider words which speak in absolutes.

Assuming that the issue is disguised, and as we know the Bar Examiners are very clever at disguise, then you still need to distinguish between answer choices. In this case, consider carefully statements that include such words as "always," "never," and "must." No doubt you learned as a first year student that there are few if any certainties in the law. For practically every rule, there is an exception—if not two or three. Use this knowledge wisely and be wary of answer choices which include words of certainty. If you can think of just one instance where it wouldn't be true, then the statement can't possibly be your best choice and you can safely eliminate it.

(5) Finally, after you've given it your best shot, move on.

With only 1.8 seconds per question, there's only so much time to allow for doubt. Remember, there will be questions that you'll find challenging and no matter how well prepared you are, they'll still present difficulty. Just don't dwell on them or you'll squander precious time that could be spent on questions you can answer.

D. SOME ADDITIONAL CONSIDERATIONS

After reading the preceding pages, it may seem to you that there are almost as many strategies for answering MBE questions as there are MBE questions themselves. But that's not exactly true. What we've focused on thus far has been development of your objective test-taking skills, a task which must account for the vagaries of the exam as well as the structure of your thought process. Although it will take considerable discipline to apply the process when answering questions initially, your speed and ability to digest and respond to questions will naturally increase as it becomes second-nature to you.

Now I'm going to tell you that notwithstanding the effectiveness of our method for rewiring your brain to answer MBE questions successfully, your approach to some MBE subjects may benefit from yet additional strategies. To be sure, the following suggestions do not rely so much on "strategy" as they do upon further consideration of the nature of the beast.

1. Individual Propensities

While the Bar Examiners accord every subject on the MBE substantially equal weight in terms of the number of questions per subject, you'll quickly find that not every subject is equal with you! I've yet to find a candidate, myself included, who was equally competent in every MBE topic. For one thing, there are some subjects that you just like better than others. You probably did well in these classes in law school and the same is likely to be the case on the bar exam. But then there are the other topics, that for whatever reason, you didn't like, couldn't understand, and simply never figured out. Maybe it was future interests, the Rule Against Perpetuities, third-party beneficiaries, intergovernmental immunities, or consequential damages. It doesn't really matter which topics they were–only that there were some that were more difficult for you. Now here they come again on the bar exam, dressed up and configured in ways that even your law professor might not recognize.

a. *When You Know Too Much*

When I started practicing questions, I was astonished to find that I was having difficulty with Contracts questions. It had been my favorite subject in law school and I even considered myself something of an "expert" in the area. I had been a Contracts Teaching Assistant and a Research Assistant for a Contracts professor. I was certainly humbled when I got question after question incorrect during my practice sessions. I started to panic. If this was the result in my supposedly "strong" subject, what chance did I have with respect to the others?

For me, it turned out that I knew the subject *too* well—I knew the exception to the exception and remembered the very language in cases. I was eliminating answer choices because they were not as precise as the holdings in cases. Here was my undoing. I knew too much! The Bar Examiners were not testing the material to this degree of exactitude. Or to put it another way, while it might have been appropriate and even critical to know the material with this degree of specificity for my professor's exam and for practice in the field, it was by no means what the bar examiners were seeking. They wanted me to know the general rules and the basic exceptions. I was making the problem more complex than it actually was because of my own sophisticated knowledge of the subject. Fortunately, I figured this out through practice and increased my percentage of correct answer choices when I stopped making the questions more complex than they were and relied instead on a general but thorough understanding of the rules. It was actually a comfort to realize that the Bar Examiners did not expect me to be an "expert" on the law but simply competent.

b.   *When You'll Never Know Enough*

On the other hand, there were some topics that eluded me in law school and eluded me still when I prepared for the bar exam. My first option, one which I heartily embraced until I saw that it wasn't at all practical, was simply to write off the offending subject. So what if I couldn't quite fathom the Rule Against Perpetuities? There weren't going to be many questions on this one topic. Then I started to conclude similarly with respect to questions in other areas that caused me difficulty: future interests and character evidence, to name but two. Suddenly I realized that while I could afford to give up a sub-topic here and there, I couldn't eliminate whole areas or I'd never pass the bar exam. I desperately needed a new strategy.

First, I decided that I would try to be as prepared as possible by making a good faith effort to review every topic. However, I also decided that this did not require that I make myself crazy when I found that even my most diligent efforts yielded minimal results. It just didn't make sense to devote hours of precious study time to a single topic which I none-theless continued to answer incorrectly.

Realizing that I didn't need a "perfect" score to pass the Multistate, I allowed myself a "pass" on my most troublesome topic. For me, it was the Rule Against Perpetuities. It simply had to go. While even the mystery of recording statutes had yielded to my efforts, I had no such luck with RAP. I felt much better about my decision after I happened to look at the Real Property subject outline in the Information Booklet and found that even the Bar Examiners had placed the Rule Against Perpetuities in a class by itself. It wasn't listed with Future Interests: it had its own place under "Special Problems."

2.   Subject–Specific Strategies

In all fairness, Future Interests and the Rule Against Perpetuities are difficult areas of the law. Not only are they conceptually complex topics, but they present long and factually dense questions. However, once I'd met my quota for concessions, I knew that I'd better figure out a way to handle other troublesome topics as they came along.

In trying to understand why certain topics presented a challenge, I realized that it wasn't simply a matter of the law. There's something about Property and Contracts questions, and Evidence ones as well. Once I started to consider these areas objectively, and not just through the haze of my own prejudices and idiosyncracies, I was able to detect a legitimate basis for my difficulties and a way to resolve them.

a. Why Contracts and Property Present a Challenge

While Contracts might have posed a difficulty for me initially because I knew too much, this subject continued to present a challenge. And I was having the same problem with some of the Property questions, quite aside from the Rule Against Perpetuities. After careful application of the forensic principles, I determined the source of the difficulty. It turns out that Contracts and Property questions share some significant characteristics—characteristics which have nothing to do with the rule of law but everything to do with the construction of the questions.

Typically, these questions are longer and feature a series of transactions between parties. Sometimes, a fact pattern can fill half of the page. And a long fact pattern generally means a greater likelihood for error—in mixing up parties, in missing significant language, and in just plain losing focus.

By realizing the source of the difficulty, I compensated for it and so can you. When a series of transactions are involved, it's essential to read the call-of-the-question first and use it to narrow the scope of the problem. Let it focus your attention on the relevant parties, cause of action, or the issue you're called upon to resolve. When you know what you're looking for, it keeps you centered as you work your way through the fact pattern. You're able to distinguish relevant from irrelevant facts, keep track of transactions, and follow the relationships between parties. And if the fact pattern contains several transactions or takes you through a series of property transfers, then by all means sketch it out in the test booklet. There's no need to keep it in your head and every reason not to!

Once you're aware of the dangers lurking in long fact patterns and how to guard against them, you're often rewarded with questions that are not nearly as difficult legally as they are to wade through factually.

b. Why Evidence Presents a Challenge

Evidence questions, on the other hand, present quite a different matter. While these questions tend to be shorter and take less time to read, they nonetheless require more time to answer. That's because each question typically involves several levels of analysis. Each analytical step takes time and presents a possibility for error.

As you no doubt recall from Evidence class when you first struggled with the rules on relevancy and character evidence, not to mention hearsay and its numerous exceptions, you learned that determining the admissibility of evidence is a multi-step process. Not only must you determine whether the evidence is admissible, but you need to assess what form that evidence is permitted to take, and sometimes, who can admit it or when it is admissible. That's a lot to consider in the span of 1.8 seconds.

Still, there's something to like about Evidence questions. They're shorter, so you can keep your focus. They require a no-nonsense direct application of the Federal Rules of Evidence. The MBE follows *only* the federal rules so don't make the common mistake of applying the rule in your particular jurisdiction or the common law rule.

And finally, remember that an Evidence question is pretty much always the same question: is this evidence admissible or inadmissible? If you identify the theory operating behind the evidentiary proffer and then apply the federal rules rigorously to the facts of the question, you're sure to end up with the right result.

c. *Statute-based Questions*

Frequently, Criminal Law questions on the MBE feature statutes. Consider these questions a gift. They're a gift because you don't have to worry about identifying which rule of law to apply to the issue—the Bar Examiners give you the rule in the statute. Statutes are a means of testing your ability to follow "the letter of the law."

Statute-based questions can be some of the easiest points you score on the MBE. The key is in knowing how to read and apply a statute to the facts. The shortest distance to the correct answer choice is a simple, direct application of the elements of the statute to the facts in the problem.

As a rule, for both statute-based and general questions, you'll want to pay particular attention to the issue of "intent." While it's easy to identify the "act" the criminal defendant committed, it's not so obvious to discern the "intent." That makes it a favorite test area of the Bar Examiners. Consequently, you should make learning the intent requirements for the different crimes a top priority when you study Criminal Law topics.

Constitutional Law questions also feature statutes but they operate a bit differently than they do in Criminal Law. Here, they're used as a vehicle to test your knowledge of federal and state powers. Typically, you'll be given a statute and asked whether it's valid. In effect, this translates to whether it's a valid exercise of the relevant state or federal power. When preparing for Constitutional Law questions, therefore, focus on learning the enumerated powers of Congress, the typical bases of state regulatory authority, and the limits on such authority. Pay particular attention to the Constitutional requirements of due process and equal protection, and everybody's favorite, the commerce clause.

d. Torts: Keep Negligence and Strict Liability "Strictly" Separate

Torts questions on the MBE are relatively "nice," rule-based questions. This means that if you know your black letter law cold, and apply the elements of the rules to the facts in the question without deviation, you should do well.

However, the Bar Examiners would not be doing their job if they didn't slip a hitch or two into the process somewhere along the line. I guess you could say that with Torts, the "problem" is that fully one half of the allotted questions deal with negligence issues. This means that you must really, truly know the categories of negligence, its elements, and the defenses. And often it's up to you to figure out that it's a negligence claim or defense from the facts of the question because the Bar Examiners won't always tell you. And just to confuse matters a bit more, they'll use words that sound in strict liability in the fact pattern and in the answer choices. Just remember that the major difference between negligence and strict liability is one of "intent" and you'll be okay. An actor can be held liable in strict liability even though he did not intend to bring about the undesirable result and even though he behaved with the utmost care. Consequently, be alert to words in the fact pattern that refer to "intent" and "care" and evaluate such language carefully against the stated cause of action. For example, if you're told that an actor "carelessly knocked a lighted Bunsen burner into a bowl of chemicals," or acted with "all reasonable care," but the suit is based in strict liability, then whether the actor was careless or careful is purely irrelevant.

E. USING FORENSICS ON THE MBE

Our use of the forensic IRAC method takes on a somewhat different cast when we apply it to objective, multiple choice questions. That's because in some way, short answer questions have already narrowed the field of possible errors. As we've learned, there are two basic skills at work on the MBE: your knowledge of the law and your ability to analyze the questions. An incorrect answer choice, therefore, must be the result of a flaw in either one of these two areas.

If you've made an error in selecting an answer choice, you must go back to that question, reread it and select another answer. However, you need to understand what you were thinking the first time around. Your task is to recreate your thought process, retrace your steps, and compare your answers in the two instances to find the flaw in your analysis. On your second read, ask yourself the following questions:

Signals for difficulties with rules:

- Am I able to identify the specific issue in controversy?
- Can I properly identify the rule of law needed to answer this issue?

Signals for difficulties with analysis:

- Am I overlooking legally significant words by reading too quickly?

- Am I reading into the question words and facts that are not there?

- Am I watching for modifiers in the answer choices?

- Am I misapplying the rule to the facts?

In this simple but highly instructive manner, you can determine whether the problem lies with your knowledge of the rule or your ability to analyze the question.

1. Was knowledge of the rule the problem?

Let's face it: if you don't know the black letter law, you can't distinguish between the answer choices. The key in analyzing the question after you've identified the issue, is to articulate the rule of law that addresses that issue. If you don't know the rule, you can't get to this step. Once again, it's not enough to know bits and pieces of rules or simply be familiar with the terminology. The Bar Examiners quickly eliminate candidates in this category.

The test in this case is straightforward: if you cannot summon to mind the relevant rule as soon as you've articulated the issue, then you must return to your notes and review the substantive law in detail. Your problem is with knowledge of the rules and you must be comfortable with answering the following questions as soon as you read a fact pattern:

- What is the legal problem presented by the facts?

- What area of law is implicated?

- What is the specific rule of law that governs under these facts?

2.   Was analysis of the question the problem?

Here, you must delve a little deeper and determine whether the problem is properly one of "reading" or of "application." If it's a reading problem, you'll find that your answer choices are incorrect because you've misread a fact somewhere in the fact pattern or answer choice. This is usually the result of sloppy reading because you're intent on reading quickly rather than carefully. A hasty reader is likely to overlook the Bar Examiners' very specific use of vocabulary and the significance of modifiers in the answer choices. Slow down and watch what happens.

If, on the other hand, you find that your errors are ones of "application," then you must consider the following:

a.   *Did you properly analyze the question:*

1.   Did you begin by reading the call-of-the-question?

2.   Did you identify the issue in the fact pattern?

3. Did you move from finding the issue to forming your answer?

4. Did you fill the gap from "your answer" to fit one of the available answer choices?

   b. Did you properly analyze the answer choices:

1. Did you identify the issue in each answer choice?

2. Did you use the process of elimination by determining when an answer choice can't be correct?

   (a) Was the answer choice completely correct?

   (b) Did the answer choice misstate or misapply a rule of law?

   (c) Did the answer choice mischaracterize the facts?

The cure for a problem in any one of these areas is practice. Answering a multiple choice question is more a science than an art. Rigor in application of the method will yield favorable results. And remember, you don't need to get them *all* right—just enough to pass.

CHAPTER 7

THE MULTISTATE PERFORMANCE TEST

A. THE PURPOSE OF THE MPT

In a perfect world, there would be no tests and a test like the bar exam would be "outlawed" instead of required for the practice of law. Short of some kind of a miracle, however, tests and the bar exam are going to be around for a while. But what would you think of an exam where the issue is identified and you're given all the law that's relevant to addressing that issue?

The good news, and you're due for some good news by now, is that the MPT can be the easiest part of your bar exam. Unlike the other portions of the exam where you're called upon to work solely from your memory, here you're given the legal issue and all the law you need to resolve the issue. You're given the law because this portion of the bar exam is designed to test your proficiency in the basic skills you've developed in the course of your legal education and not just your ability to memorize. According to the National Conference of Bar Examiners, the goal of the MPT is to test "an applicant's ability to use fundamental lawyering skills in a

189

realistic situation." Each test, therefore, seeks to evaluate your ability to complete a task which a beginning lawyer should be able to accomplish.

The sum total of your law school experience has prepared you for this part of the bar exam. It just does so in a way that looks different because the MPT puts all the elements together in a manner that is new to students who have not yet had the opportunity to work with case files and clients. However, having worked with case files and clients, I can assure you there no mystery to it nor any substitute for proficiency in the most basic of skills.

But now that I've told you about the positive part about the exam, I must be fair and tell you about the negative. And just like there's always an opposing argument, there's always a downside. Here it's the time pressure. In most jurisdictions, you have but 90 minutes to read through anywhere from 15 to 25 pages, analyze the problem, outline your answer, and write your response. In California, where the MPT is a three-hour exam, you can just imagine the length of the file and the number of issues to which you must respond. As a result, the MPT is basically a test of your ability to work within time constraints and remain organized and focused.

Still, the MPT remains the most "doable" portion of the bar exam. It's not difficult "legally." The challenge is to get through the pile of information you are given and address only that which is required of you as set forth in the task memo. What we're going to do is develop the strategy you'll use when taking this part of the bar exam. Your goal is to make your approach to the material so mechanical that come test day, it's pure routine.

B.   THE SKILLS TESTED ON THE MPT

On the MPT, the bar examiners are interested in testing your fundamental lawyering skills. The focus is on your ability to comprehend what you read, organize information, think logically, extricate the relevant from the irrelevant, write clearly, and above all, follow directions.

1.   *Reading Comprehension*

First, you'll be called upon to read. But there's a very real difference between the type of reading you've engaged in for your law school classes and what you'll do for the MPT. Here you must read pro-actively, with a critical eye toward solving a specific problem rather than answering a professor's questions in class. You must read carefully and quickly, all the while searching for useful information and answers to the particular issue you've been asked to resolve.

2.   *Organizational Skills*

Second, you must organize your time and the materials effectively to complete the required task in the time allowed. The MPT is extremely time-sensitive, perhaps even more so than the essay or multiple choice components of the bar exam in that you'll have but 90 minutes in which to read and analyze an assortment of unfamiliar materials and compose any one of the following written assignments—a memorandum of law, a letter to a client, a persuasive brief (including subject headings), a contract provision, a will, a proposal for settlement, a discovery plan, or a closing argument, to list but a few of the possibilities.

3. Communication Skills

Third, you must be able to write concisely, coherently, and in a tone and manner consistent with the nature of the assignment. In short, you must demonstrate your mastery of the language of the law and convince the bar examiners that you "sound" like an attorney ready to begin the practice of law.

4. Ability to Follow Directions

Finally, you must be able to follow directions. It sounds so simple and basic but it's often ignored in the haste to begin writing. The MPT is task-specific: you must perform the task identified to receive credit. If you're instructed to write a letter to a client and instead write a persuasive brief, you'll have done nothing but demonstrate to the bar examiners your inability to read and follow simple directions.

The directions on the MPT are important for yet another reason: they may ask you to identify *additional* facts that would strengthen or, alternatively, weaken a party's position. Since adding facts to a professor's hypothetical is a basic law school "no-no," you'd never think to do such a thing—not unless you had read the directions. The ability to follow directions closely will save you time and energy, both on the bar exam and in practice.

C. HOW THESE SKILLS ARE TESTED

The bar examiners test these skills by simulating the experiences of a new attorney. You'll be given a "client file" and asked to complete what would be considered a typical assignment for a first year associate. Each assignment is designed to test a discrete set of legal skills in the context of one of the following settings:

- Fact-based tasks
- Discovery-type tasks
- Analytical tasks
- Meeting client goals
- Ethical conflicts

1. *"Analyzing the facts"*

In this type of problem, you'll be called upon to analyze a set of facts where the primary focus will be to separate the relevant from the irrelevant. Here the rules of law will serve to help you organize the facts.

Such tasks might include:

- Drafting an opening statement
- Drafting a closing argument
- Preparing a set of jury instructions
- Writing an affidavit

I can practically hear you thinking—"I've never done that. I'd have no idea what to do. And you said that this was the most doable part of the exam!" Not to worry. The bar examiners do not expect you to have performed all or even any of these tasks during your law school career. What they do expect, however, is that you'll be able to follow their instruction memo and rely on your basic legal training to complete the assignment.

If you think about it, performing these kinds of tasks can be something of a welcome change from the rest of the exam. After all, you get to "perform" like a lawyer, albeit on paper. Can't you just imagine yourself delivering an opening statement like: "Ladies and Gentlemen of the Jury. The prosecution must prove all four of the following elements beyond a reasonable doubt before you can find my client guilty of this crime. Reasonable doubt requires that...."

What comes next? A statement to the jury that the testimony they're about to hear won't support the elements of the crime so that they'll have to find your client "not guilty." Your opening statement will discuss the facts of the case but you'll organize that discussion around the elements of the crime.

2.   *"Discovering the facts"*

Fact gathering is a basic lawyering task. It requires that you be able to identify the theory of your case and what facts you need to prove to make that case. Consequently, in a typical discovery-type problem, you'll be required to gather evidence. The focus will be on sifting through information to determine what's relevant to your problem and then using that evidence to defend or support your case.

Typical tasks include:

- Drafting a discovery plan

- Preparing a set of interrogatories

- Drafting questions to ask a witness on cross examination

"Discovery" tasks, like "fact-based" tasks, test your ability to use the rule to discriminate between relevant and irrelevant facts. For example, while the focus in drafting a set of interrogatories is on questions to elicit facts, you must understand and use the controlling rule to determine what facts you need to gather.

3. *"Legal reasoning"*

Happily, in this type of problem, you'll feel right at home. Here, the focus will be on analyzing the rules of law from the cases and applying them to the facts in your File to resolve the legal issue. Sound familiar? These problems are most like law school exams but with a major difference: the MPT will articulate the precise legal issue(s) for you. You just need to follow directions carefully and answer the precise question that is asked of you.

Typical tasks include:

- Writing an objective memorandum

- Writing a persuasive memorandum of law or trial brief
- Writing a client letter
- Writing a letter to opposing counsel

4.   *"Meeting client goals"*

In this type of assignment, you'll be called upon to evaluate courses of action and outline viable options. The focus is on your ability to develop strategies for solving a problem and meeting your client's needs. You may even be called upon to suggest such non-legal solutions as mediation or counseling.

Examples of problem-solving tasks include:

- Drafting a will or contract provision to meet specific client objectives
- Drafting a settlement proposal or separation agreement to address specified goals

5.   *"Ethical conflicts"*

As a bar candidate, you're expected to comport with the applicable ethical standards in your representation of a client. Consequently, you may find ethical issues raised in your problem. You're expected to recognize such issues and resolve them according to the ethical standards of the profession. Conceivably, the bar examiners could raise an ethical issue without providing specific rules in the Library; in such cases, you must rely on your general knowledge of the rules of professional conduct. Be alert in your reading of the facts to potential conflict of interest issues, violations of fiduciary obligations, and breaches of attorney/client privilege.

D.   COMPONENTS OF THE MPT

The MPT consists of the following parts:

1.   *The File*

The File contains all the factual information about your case. It may consist of such documents as excerpts from deposition testimony, client correspondence, police reports, medical records, invoices, purchase orders, witness interviews, contract provisions, a lease, or a will. While the File contains all the facts you need to know about your problem, it also contains "irrelevant information." Just as in "real life" where your client will volunteer much more information than you actually need or is relevant to the legal problem, and witnesses may be unreliable or have faulty memories, the File may include irrelevant or ambiguous information, unreliable and conflicting witness testimony, and inconsistent statements.

2.   *The "Task" or "Action" Memorandum*

This is the single most important document in the File because it contains your directions. It is the first memorandum in the File and introduces your problem. After reading this memo, you'll know whether you are to write an objective memorandum, a persuasive brief, a client letter, or any one of a number of other tasks. Your goal will be to answer the questions posed in this memo and perform the assigned task as precisely as possible.

3. *The Library*

The Library contains all the legal authorities you'll need to complete the assigned task. And it contains the ***only*** legal authorities you may use to solve the problem. While outside knowledge is useful to guide your understanding of the law, you must rely solely on the law presented in the Library.

The Library may consist of statutes, codes and commentaries, constitutional provisions, regulations, rules of professional conduct, cases, and secondary sources such as Restatement provisions. The cases may be actual cases, modified cases, or cases written specifically for the exam. So too with the "rules"—they may be actual rules or rules written specifically for the MPT. This means that even if you think you are familiar with a rule or a case from your law school classes, you must still read all the material in the Library. You cannot assume that the material has not been modified. Certainly, there may be rules that the bar examiners have not altered, such as the UCC, provisions of the United States Constitution, the Bill of Rights, or the Federal Rules of Evidence. In these instances, the directions will so advise.

If no Library is provided, then any law necessary to resolving the problem will be provided in the File.

E. STRATEGIES FOR SUCCESS ON THE MPT

1. *Having a Plan*

In working with students to prepare for the MPT, I've put together a set of guidelines that students found helpful and subsequently used as a blueprint to guide them through the problems during practice sessions and on test day. Following this plan saves time and prevents panic: if you know what you are going to do, and practice the routine sufficiently, it becomes second nature to you by test day.

2. *Practicing from Actual MPTs*

Like the other parts of the bar exam, preparing for the MPT requires practice. Still, preparation for the MPT is unlike preparation for the other parts of the bar exam. Here you're not tested so much on your knowledge of black letter law as you are on your ability to extract legal principles from cases and statutes and apply these principles to solve a specific client problem. The commercial bar preparation courses provide a comprehensive review of the substantive law. Unfortunately, such courses are not designed to cultivate the analytical and writing skills you need on the MPT. These are the skills you should have developed in law school and these are the skills you must fine tune on your own.

Reprints of the MPT questions and a discussion of the issues and suggested resolutions of the problems as contemplated by the drafters of the MPT are available from the National Conference of Bar

Examiners. They have prepared grading sheets which describe the issues the candidate should discuss and the grading guidelines. While the point sheets are very helpful in identifying the issues you need to address in your answer and their corresponding point allocation, the point sheets do not provide the words themselves. Individual jurisdictions may release candidate answers just as they do for essays. If your jurisdiction releases sample MPT answers, be sure to review them as carefully as you do sample essay answers. For many students, the overriding concern is just how to get started: how to write the opening sentence, the point headings, and the case summaries. Your first task is to acquire a good number of available MPTs and only then are you ready to begin. I would suggest a minimum of six.

3.   *Following the Blueprint*

The strategy for success is simple: you practice the following approach until it becomes automatic. Follow each step of the sequence for each MPT— first as you practice, and then on test day. The goal is for this process to become so mechanical that you do not waste any time but get to work immediately. You remain calm because you always know what your next step will be.

Let's get to work.

a.   *Read the Instructions*

There is an instruction sheet on the back of every MPT. Read it in its entirety *now*. You don't want to waste time on exam day performing a routine task you can do beforehand. However, on bar day, you'll scan the instruction sheet just to make sure it's the same one you've read during practice—you don't want any surprises. You'll pay particular attention to paragraph 2 and read it carefully to verify the jurisdiction.

The instructions are straightforward but pay careful attention to the following:

(1) **Paragraph 2:** defines the jurisdiction of the MPT

The MPT is set in the fictitious Fifteenth Circuit of the United States, in the fictitious State of Franklin. In Franklin, the trial court is the District Court, the intermediate appellate court is the Court of Appeal, and the highest court is the Supreme Court.

On the MPT, as in practice, you must know the court structure before you read the cases so you can determine what is mandatory and what is merely persuasive authority.

(2) **Paragraph 4:** describes the Library

Occasionally, cases may seem familiar to you. The examiners may have patterned the case after a famous case. You are instructed not to assume any knowledge but to read thoroughly as if all were new to you. You are also told to assume that the cases were decided in the jurisdictions and on the dates shown. What are the bar examiners

really telling you? They are telling you that jurisdiction and case dates are significant because:

  (i) "Jurisdiction" tells you what is *mandatory*
      as opposed to what is merely *persuasive*
      authority.

  (ii) "Case dates" may be a way of determining
       whether the more recent case overruled the
       earlier case.

(3) **Paragraph 5:** some advice

You are advised to work ***only*** from the facts in
the File and the law in Library.

(4) **Paragraph 6:** suggested time allocation

The bar examiners suggest that you spend half
your time on reading and outlining and half your
time on writing. You could go five (5) or so
minutes either way but you should not spend less
than 40 minutes on either task. It's simply insufficient to get the job done.

(5) **Paragraph 7:** What the examiners are look-
    ing for

  (i) Responsiveness to the instructions in the
      task

  (ii) Content

  (iii) Thoroughness

  (iv) Organization of response

Note that fully one-half the available points are
not so much about the substance of what you've
written but whether you've answered the question
that is asked of you and organized your response in

a meaningful manner. This reinforces the importance the bar examiners place on your ability to remain focused and structured in your response.

b. *Review the Table of Contents*

Use the Table of Contents to begin your *"active reading"* of the MPT.

From this page, you can identify:

(1) **Whether it's a statutory or a common law problem.**

If you have a common law problem, which will be obvious when all you have are cases in your Library, then it's likely that you'll have a bit more work to do; typically, you'll have to synthesize the applicable rule from the cases.

(2) **The area of law.**

From the listings in the Library, you can determine the general subject area, sometimes more. For example, if you see provisions of the Franklin Commercial Code listed in the Table of Contents, it's a sure bet you have a problem involving a sales of goods.

(3) **Don't let the area of law cause needless worry or anxiety.**

Examiners may choose an unfamiliar area of law or one that you don't particularly like. In such cases, the key is not to let the subject matter distract you. You'll be given all the relevant law you need to solve the problem so even if it happens to be an area of law in which you think you're weak, it doesn't matter. And if it's an unfamiliar area of law, the bar examiners know that too and the problem will be relatively basic and solvable by using the provided materials.

c.   *Read the Task Memo*

This is the *single most important document* in the File for the following reasons:

(1) **It introduces your problem**

The task memo provides the relevant background facts, introduces the parties, and sets forth the nature of your task.

(2) **It states your issue**

The task memo reveals the precise issue you're asked to resolve. It may appear in the form of the questions you're asked to address in a client letter, in the argument you need to make in a brief, or even in the supervising attorney's theory of the case.

Read this portion of the memo two or three times to be certain you have identified the issue. Write the issue on your scratch paper so that you remain focused as you proceed. Be careful not to change or vary the language of the question.

Most jurisdictions will provide scratch paper. If not, carefully follow the directions on the instruction sheet as to where you're allowed to write your notes.

(3) **It contains your directions**

Read the directions very carefully. The bar examiners may request that you do more than simply analyze the facts in light of the relevant law and write an objective evaluation; they may request that you identify additional facts that would strengthen a party's position, state the most persuasive arguments that can be made to support a given position, or identify likely outcomes.

Look for exclusions.

Sometimes you are told **not** to consider a specific issue. In these cases, the issue would most likely jump out at you when you read the problem and your first response would be to discuss it. **Your job is not to discuss it.** Fight the desire to do so because the graders are lying in wait to take off points for those who fail to follow basic instructions.

(4) **It identifies your task**

You will be told whether to write an objective memorandum, a persuasive brief, a client letter, or any one of a number of other possibilities.

From your task, you should:

(i) *Identify your point of view: is it objective or persuasive?*

You want to know whether you will be advising or advocating. This informs the nature of your reading because you'll read the materials with a critical eye. For example, if you know you must write a persuasive brief with subject headings, you'll read the cases with an eye toward formulating them.

(ii) *Identify your audience: lay or legal?*

You want to know your audience because it allows you to adopt the proper tone in your writing. Whether you are to write an objective evaluation or a persuasive argument determines how you will approach the materials in your File.

d.   Review the Guideline Memo (if applicable)

If the examiners think you need guidance in completing your task, they'll include a second memo in the File. There are guidelines for opinion letters, persuasive briefs, memorandums, etc. Each memo will tell you exactly what to include (and sometimes what *not* to include) in your paper. Be sure to follow these guidelines to the letter.

For example, the guideline memo will advise you whether your persuasive brief requires a statement of facts or not. A "persuasive brief" might require a factual statement while a "trial brief" might not. Sometimes you might be asked to include a "jurisdictional statement" as well as a statement of facts. Only a careful reading of the guideline memo will ensure that you know what to include in your assignment. Even if the guideline memo specifies a task you think you know well, ***do not*** skip the guideline sheet. Sometimes the examiners have modified the task or require a particular format.

In addition to providing general guidelines, sometimes this sheet will include specific examples for you to follow in drafting your document. Such examples might be sample interrogatories, will and contract provisions, jury instructions, and questions for cross-examination, to name a few. The examples are included for a very good reason: they are your "models." Follow them!

An important part of your preparation for the MPT is to read these memos now and be completely familiar with them so that on test day you need spend only a few precious moments reviewing them before proceeding. You must check the guideline memo even if it seems familiar because it's never safe to assume that it's identical to one you've seen in practice.

e. Read the Library

Although the first part of the exam booklet is the File, this is not where you'll begin. Instead, you're going to begin with the Library.

Reading the law first informs your subsequent reading of the File. If you read the File first, with its various excerpts from depositions, client communications, and attorney notes, it would be more difficult, if not impossible, to sift relevant from irrelevant information. You simply could not know which facts were "relevant" until you knew the law and how the cases in your jurisdiction have interpreted that law. While reading the Library first does not guarantee you won't have to review it again, it will make your subsequent reading of the File meaningful and immediately productive.

Caution: Irrelevant rules

There may be some authorities in the Library that are irrelevant to your analysis. Clearly, you won't know what is or is not relevant at this point. You must wait to make that judgment until after you've read the facts in the File. What's important to remember is that there might be "law" in the Library that won't be applicable to your analysis. Let your issue and the facts be your guide.

Follow this sequence:

(1) **Read the cases**

Read the earliest case first and proceed in chronological order.

Sometimes, just as in the real world, the later case will modify the holding in the earlier case or it will build on the ruling in the earlier case. Often, the cases are not related but you won't know until you've read them. Then it doesn't matter which you've read first. It's just easier to get in the habit of always beginning with the earliest case.

Reading the cases in the Library tends to be the most time-consuming part of the MPT. Even if you're a fast reader, it will still consume too much of your time if you read these cases like you did in law school. Instead, you're going to read like a practitioner. Practicing attorneys read cases to find what they need from them: the rule of law in their jurisdiction and the basic facts. Therefore, when you read a case, you will:

(i) **Verify the jurisdiction.**

Immediately check the jurisdiction of the decision to determine the authority of the case. Assess whether it's mandatory or merely persuasive. Pay attention to the jurisdiction of cases cited by courts in their decisions: sometimes they will discuss other cases. Once again, you need to know whether or not you must follow that ruling.

(ii) **Identify the rule of law.**

The cases are the means by which the examiners feed you the law. Sometimes, they'll be so blunt as to have the court state something like, "During the past 30 years, we have developed a two-pronged analysis for evaluating the validity of a premarital agreement."

Such a statement is a "gift"—it gives you the rule and its two elements. Sometimes, your gift will not appear in the form of a rule with "prongs." In such cases, the elements will be listed as the requirements of a crime or they'll appear in a statute. Simply break the statute into its component elements and proceed accordingly.

(iii) **Skim the facts to get a sense of the story.**

On the MPT, the cases are constructed in a very particular order: facts, rule, and application of facts to rule. MPT cases closely resemble actual cases. Therefore, you can read the first few words of each paragraph and you'll know exactly where you are. Consider skipping the first few paragraphs and jump right to the rule. If you're insecure about skipping around, then read the entire case but merely skim the facts quickly. You can pick up the relevant facts from the court's application.

(iv) **Read the footnotes.**

Footnotes hold a special place in the hearts of bar examiners because they know that students tend to ignore them. That's why bar examiners like to put them in cases. Don't ignore them. They are there for a reason. More than half the time, they contain critical information.

(2) **Use the rule of law to form your outline**

Adapt the rule to form your "mini working outline." Use the elements, the "prongs" of a rule, or the components of a statute to form the roman numerals of your outline. A general outline is then in place as you read the rest of the Library. You can add to and refine your understanding of the rule as well as add any exceptions or limitations to the rule as you read the other materials in the Library.

When you read your File, you can do either of the following:

1. Simply add your "facts" in the space beneath the appropriate rule.

    Or

2. Create a *parallel set of point headings* where you'll note the facts from your case that correspond to each of the elements of the rule.

If you create this outline when you first find the rule, you'll have prepared the foundation for writing your assigned task.

(3) **Read the statutes, codes, commentaries**

Pay close attention to any "official comments" in a statute or code provision. Such comments are a means for the bar examiners to highlight an issue, draw your attention to a counter-argument, or signal a legal distinction.

Outlining the Rule from Cases

Let's see how it's done. Look at Test 2 of the February 1997, MPT, *In re Hayworth and Wexler*. Here the Library contains a case, *In the Matter of Watson*, and several provisions of the Franklin Professional Code. The court in *Watson* tells you when a premarital agreement will be found valid and binding in the State of Franklin:

> During the past 30 years, we have developed a two-pronged analysis for evaluating the validity of a premarital agreement. *Under the first prong, the court must decide whether the agreement provides a fair and reasonable provision for the party not seeking enforcement of the agreement.* If the court makes this finding, then the analysis ends and the agreement may be validated. *If the agreement is not fair, the court must invoke the second prong and decide: (A) whether full disclosure has been made by the parties of the amount, character, and value of the property involved, and (B) whether the agreement was entered into intelligently*

and voluntarily on independent advice and with full knowledge by both spouses of their rights. (Emphasis added to indicate rule)

Use this statement to create your outline. The court lays it out for you: it tells you there's a two-part rule and then it further divides the second prong into two parts, A and B. Your outline should look something like this:

I.   Agreement must be **fair and reasonable** for the party not seeking enforcement

What is "fair and reasonable"?

a.   Not when "grossly disproportionate" in favor of petitioner

b.   Not when it denies party common law and statutory rights

c.   Not when it prevents party from making any claim against or seeking any rights in husband's separate property

Note: When a court uses such terms as "fair and reasonable," rely on the factors it considers in its evaluation and use them as your criteria. In this case, sub-points a, b, and c were the specific factors the Watson court considered in evaluating whether the prenup was fair and reasonable.

If fair, then enforceable.

II.   If not fair, ask

A.   Was there full disclosure of

(1) **amount,**

(2) **character,** and

(3) **value** of the property

and

B.   Was the agreement entered into

(1) **intelligently**

(2) **voluntarily**

(3) on **independent advice** and

(4) with **full knowledge by both spouses of their rights**

Your outline shouldn't be any longer or wordier than this. Underline or highlight the key words to help you remember them as you read the File. As you can see, the factors in the second part of the test are so clear as to not require additional explanation. You can simply "match" up the facts in your case with the requirements of the test.

If you've left space under each part of the rule, you can simply write in your facts or you can create a parallel set of point headings. It really doesn't matter so long as it is perfectly clear to you.

This outline is invaluable to you. It ensures that you won't leave out any elements when you begin your analysis, an oversight that's quite easy to make under the extreme pressure of exam writing.

I devised this technique when one of the students I was working with failed to include the first prong of the rule in his analysis of this problem. It seems that in his eagerness to write his answer, he overlooked the first part of the rule and referred only to sub-parts A and B in his analysis. He told me that he had trouble making sense of the problem but when he reviewed the case, he saw that it was supposed to be a two-part rule and thought that parts A and B were the two parts. That is when he realized the value of preparing an outline. And, so will you.

f. Read the File

After you've read the Library and outlined the rule, you're ready to return to the File and add the relevant facts to the appropriate places in your outline.

Don't be surprised if you find yourself reading a fair amount of material that you believe is irrelevant. As you may recall from writing your Statement of Facts in legal memos and briefs, you need to include more than the "bare bones" in your factual statement to provide the reader with the necessary background information. Consequently, you'll be faced with what seems like an avalanche of information as you proceed. It will be more manageable if you follow this advice:

(1) **Write the issue above your outline.** By reading the File with the issue clearly in place, you can more easily identify the legally relevant facts from the sea of material in front of you. As you proceed, add the critical facts to the appropriate part of your outline. By now you should have a clear picture of the problem and how you can resolve it.

(2) **Characterize the legal relationship of the parties and your client.** Are they buyer and seller, teacher and student, husband and wife, employer and employee? By thinking of the parties in terms of their legal relationship to each other, you'll be alert to the legal significance of the facts contained in the depositions, transcripts, and correspondence.

g. *Reread the Task Memo*

After you've written the outline, review the task memo. Ask the following questions:

- Has my outline incorporated or accounted for each required element?
- Are the relevant facts noted?
- Is the applicable legal authority cited?
- Do I account for how the law and the facts support my theory?
- If appropriate, has contrary authority been cited and distinguished?

If necessary, add to the outline.

h. *Review the Guideline Memo*

Quickly check the memo once again to verify your task and the required components.

i. *Write your Response*

After completing your reading of the Library and File, you're ready to begin the task of writing. Remember, your job is to discuss the issues and the controlling rule of law. Here is where you get your points. Don't waste time "warming up" by reciting the facts or providing needless background information.

(1) **Adopt the tone and format required for your task.**

For example, if you're asked to write a client letter, you must adapt your writing style accordingly. This means that you recognize your reader is a layperson and if you use any legal terms in your letter, you'll explain such terms in a manner that an ordinary citizen would comprehend. Also, you'll want your assignment to resemble a letter so you'll include a mock letterhead and an introductory statement. Even though it's a letter, you'll want to guide your reader (and the grader) through your analysis so use sub-headings to separate the issues.

Your letter might begin something like the following example which is based on the July 1997, MPT, *In re Kiddie–Gym Systems, Inc.*:

Jerome A. Martin, President
Kiddie–Gym Systems, Inc.
4722 Industrial Way
Bradley Center, FN 33087

RE: Loss by Fire of Installed Playground Equipment at Bradley Center Shopping Mall

Dear Mr. Martin,

I am writing to respond to your inquiries concerning the liability of your company, KGS, for the loss of the playground equipment. I've reviewed the applicable law and the following is our opinion with respect to the issues we've discussed.

Risk of Loss

The first issue is whether your company bears the risk of loss for the playground equipment destroyed in the fire at Cornet's Bradley Center Shopping Mall.

Similarly, if you're asked to write an objective memorandum of law, you'll assume a neutral tone and objectively evaluate the facts in light of the applicable law. Alternatively, if you're asked to write a legal brief or any form of argument, you'll adopt the tone of an advocate and use forceful and persuasive language.

(2) **Write Persuasive Subject Headings**

Perhaps the most challenging task for candidates is when they're asked to include subject headings in their argument. Most students have not had the opportunity or the need to write subject headings since their first year of law school. And if you're like most students, you struggled through it and promptly forget about it. Unfortunately, commercial bar prep courses are not going to teach you how to do this because there isn't time and quite simply, it's not their job. Still, you have the opportunity to rack up considerable points with just a few sentences.

Let's be honest: a grader is inclined to look favorably upon a paper that immediately sets forth the proper tone and has apparently followed directions. For the bar examiners don't leave it to chance that you'll write effective subject headings: they give specific directions on what they want and what they don't want. The instruction memo for the July 1997, MPT, *State v. Devine*, provides the following example:

Improper: THE WITNESS IS COMPETENT TO TESTIFY.

Proper: A FIVE–YEAR–OLD WHO ADMITTED HER MOTHER WOULD NOT PUNISH HER FOR LYING, BUT STILL TESTIFIED SHE KNEW THAT LYING WAS WRONG, IS COMPETENT TO TESTIFY.

The key to writing an effective subject heading is simple:

State the legal conclusion you want the court to reach and the factual basis on which it can do so.

I drafted the following sample point headings. They address the two issues for the trial brief on evidentiary proffers you're asked to prepare for *State v. Devine*.

I. THE TESTIMONY OF AN EXPERIENCED POLICE DETECTIVE WHO WITNESSED THE DEFENDANT SELLING COCAINE BUT TWO DAYS BEFORE THE DEFENDANT'S CURRENT ARREST FOR COCAINE POSSESSION SHOULD BE ADMITTED AS PROOF OF INTENT.

II. WHERE THE DEFENDANT WAS CONVICTED EIGHTEEN MONTHS AGO FOR POSSESSION OF HEROIN WITH INTENT TO DISTRIBUTE, SERVED A YEAR IN PRISON, AND HAS BEEN RELEASED ONLY SIX MONTHS BEFORE HIS CURRENT ARREST FOR THE SAME OFFENSE, EVIDENCE OF THE CONVICTION SHOULD BE ADMISSIBLE TO SHOW INTENT.

The following are some guidelines to writing subject headings:

- The purpose of point headings is to provide the reader with an outline of your argument.

- Each point heading is written as a conclusory statement that combines the law with the relevant facts.

- It should be a coherent, logical, and persuasive thesis sentence.

- Do not state abstract principles of law.

- Do not write objective, neutral statements.

- If your adversary would agree with your statement, then you haven't written it right.

The good news is that if you practice writing point headings now as you prepare from the practice MPTs, they will flow from your pen on test day.

(3) **Write Effective Case Summaries**

Another important skill to review and practice before test day is writing case summaries. A common error is to write summaries of what the cases are about instead of simply reducing a case to its core facts, holding, and reasoning. Typically, you've not written case analyses on law school exams and unless you've written legal papers or worked on one of your school's journals, chances are that your only exposure to writing such summaries was in your first year legal writing class.

Your goal on the MPT is not to write a case brief or even a lengthy analysis but to concisely state the holding and facts of the Library case and then compare that case to the facts of your case.

When working with the Library, the most common error is to include long passages and quotations from the cases in your text. *Do not do this!* It adds nothing to your legal argument (and no points) but adds tremendously to your writing time. Instead, focus on the facts, holding, and reasoning of the opinion and write something like this:

> "In *Lopez*, the court held that the school board acted constitutionally when it required profanity be deleted from a student-produced film before it could be shown. The court reasoned that the school board had not censored the students' expression of ideas but prohibited the use of profanity in expressing those ideas and thus the board's requirement was content neutral and served a valid pedagogical purpose." *Lopez v. Union High School District.*

Here, you've provided the holding in the case, its factual basis, and the reasoning the court relied

upon in reaching that decision—and all in two
sentences!

(4) **Use Effective Case Analysis**

Equally important is to give adequate treatment
to the cases in the Library. The bar examiners
expect you to apply the rule from these cases to
the specific facts in your case. For example, in the
July 1999, MPT, *Kantor v. Bellows*, you're asked
to write a letter to your adversary explaining why
your client is entitled to the equitable distribution
of her husband's law degree and license to practice law. One requirement is that you include a
specific dollar demand and justify that amount. In
responding to this request, you might consider
the following to show how you've used the materials in the Library to support your argument:

> "Linda is entitled to a distributive award of $335,000
> as compensation for her contributions to Bill's degree
> and enhanced earning capacity."

After explaining how you arrived at this figure,
you'd explain its legal justification:

> "In determining the disposition of property in divorce
> actions, the court considers several factors such as
> the income and property of each party at the time of
> marriage and at the time of the commencement of
> the action, and the direct and indirect contributions
> made to the acquisition of marital property, including
> the career of the other party. Section 5, Franklin
> Domestic Relations Law. While the Franklin Court of
> Appeal in *Sooke v. Sooke* made a distributive award
> to the wife of only 40% of the value of the husband's
> medical degree, the facts in that case are not as
> compelling as the ones in our case. Here, Linda is

> entitled to one-half of the value of Bill's enhanced
> earning capacity because the parties agreed that both
> would have the opportunity to pursue legal careers
> and that Linda would work while Bill attended law
> school first.''

You can see how easily it would be to continue
with the relevant facts from the File and compare
and contrast with the facts from *Sooke*. Clearly,
this is more than a superficial analysis and you've
developed your argument by synthesizing the applicable law and the facts from your case.

(5) **Citation**

On the MPT, as in practice, you must "cite" to
the relevant authority. However, "official" cita-
tion form is not required for the MPT. Simply use
abbreviations and omit page references. With
cases, a reference to the plaintiff's or defendant's
name is sufficient. Your goal is to attribute an
authority for your statement, thus demonstrating
to the grader that you've used the Library effectively and that you're familiar with the need for
proper legal documentation.

F.   TIME IS OF THE ESSENCE

1.   Allocating your Time

While I've left the matter of timing to the end, it
may well be the most important point to consider.
Clearly, you must complete the assignment to maximize your points. The bar examiners suggest that
you allot 45 minutes to reading the materials and
45 minutes to organizing and writing your re-

sponse. This is sound advice. Moreover, if you follow the strategies I've outlined, you'll be organizing your response while you're reading the materials, thereby maximizing your productivity.

2.   Finding Your Baseline

Of course, you can have no real idea of how long any of this will take unless and until you've done it. Therefore, after you've read one or two of the MPTs to get a sense of what they're about, select another one and just read and outline the materials, practicing the techniques you've just learned. Note how long it takes you to do this. This is your baseline *reading and outlining* time. Then, proceed to write the response. Once again, time yourself. This is your baseline *writing* time. Do not be surprised or disheartened if it seems to take several hours to get through the materials. This is normal the first time you approach new material. Still, the experience will be somewhat different for everyone. Some read faster than others; others have difficulty writing. You need to learn how long it takes you to perform each of these tasks.

Once you've established your reading and writing baselines, you can concentrate on improving your time. Learning to allocate your time is a challenging but not insurmountable task. You can do it with practice. You must practice the strategy until it becomes automatic and your approach is consistent. Don't wait until test day to see how long it takes you to dissect a case for the rule and prepare a response. ***You'd never wait until the day of your road test to practice parallel parking, would you?***

G. BAR EXAMINATION MPT CHECK-LIST

Follow the Blueprint:

I.   Reviewing the Instructions

   1.   Did you scan the paragraphs to verify the requirements?

   2.   Did you verify the jurisdiction paragraph to know what is *mandatory* as opposed to what is merely *persuasive* authority?

II.   Reviewing the Table of Contents

   1.   Did you identify the general area of law?

   2.   Did you determine whether it's a statutory or common law problem?

III.   Reading the Task Memo

   1.   Did you identify the issue you're asked to resolve? Are there sub-issues?

   2.   Did you identify your specific assignment by

      a)   Noting the precise nature of the task: memo, brief, letter, contract provision, will provision, cross examination questions, etc.

      b)   Identifying your point of view: is it objective or persuasive?

      c)   Identifying your audience: is it a lawyer or layperson?

   3.   Did you note any exclusions?

IV. Reading the Guideline Memo

1. Did you note whether a particular format or structure is required?

2. If a brief was requested, do you need to include

    a) A statement of facts?

    b) A jurisdictional statement?

    c) Persuasive subject headings?

3. Are there specific examples/models to follow?

V. Reading the Library

1. Did you read the cases first?

2. For each case, did you

    a) Read the earliest case first and proceed chronologically?

    b) Verify the jurisdiction to determine whether it's mandatory or persuasive authority for your problem?

    c) Skim the facts to get a sense of the story?

    d) Identify the statement of the rule?

        ● Is it element-based?

        ● Do you need to synthesize from the cases?

        ● Is it a "multi-part test" formulated by the court?

    e) Note any footnotes?

2. Did you adapt the rule in the cases to form your outline?

3. Did you review the statutes, codes, commentaries

VI. Reading the File

1. Did you begin by

   a) Writing your issue above your rule outline?

   b) Characterizing the legal relationship of the parties: Are they buyer and seller, teacher and student, husband and wife, employer and employee, attorney and client?

2. Did you identify the relevant facts based on your knowledge of the law from the Library?

3. Did you add these facts to the appropriate sections of your rule outline?

VII. Preparing to Write

1. Did you review the task and guideline memos to verify the issue and the task?

2. Has your outline incorporated each required element?

   a) the applicable legal authority?

   b) the relevant facts?

VIII. Writing the Response

1. Did you answer the question that was asked of you?

2. Did you adopt the tone and format required for the task?

3. Did you write persuasive subject headings?

- Did you state the legal conclusion you want the court to reach and the factual basis on which it can do so?

- Is each point heading written as a conclusory statement that combines the law with the relevant facts?

- Is it a coherent, logical, and persuasive thesis sentence?

- Have you avoided abstract principles of law?

- Would your adversary agree with your statement?

4. Did you give adequate treatment to the cases in the Library?

5. Did you avoid copying passages from cases or statutes?

6. Did you make relevant arguments on how the law and the facts support your theory?

7. Has contrary authority been cited and distinguished?

8. Did you cite to the appropriate authorities for statements of the rule?

CHAPTER 8

IF AT FIRST YOU DIDN'T SUCCEED

A. ADVICE FOR THE RE–TAKER

It might be said that you face the most daunting task of all: overcoming your fear of failure. My heart is with you. But I know that you can pass the bar exam because I've worked with countless re-takers to know that it's possible. It's possible because you're going to follow the plan this time.

There are any number of reasons candidates don't pass the bar exam: the reasons are almost as varied as the test takers themselves. There are always a small minority of candidates who walk into the exam unprepared, knowing that they're unprepared. But this isn't typical. The vast majority work hard in preparing for the exam but working hard is not the same as working smart.

It won't be easy to pick up your books once again, but pick them up you must if you want to be the attorney you went to law school to become. Allow yourself some time to regroup emotionally and physically before taking up the task of bar preparation once again. But once you do, don't look back! You're not the same person you were the first time around, and now you're going to do things very differently.

And you must proceed differently to achieve a different result. Some re-takers erroneously believe that if they had simply spent more time on their studies, they would have passed. However, I can practically guarantee that spending more time doing what you've done before will do nothing to change the outcome. A different result requires a different approach, not more of the same.

As we've discussed throughout this book, mastering the bar exam is not just a function of time but the development of some very specific test-taking skills, a task which must account for the nature of the exam and the structure of your thought process. In fact, because you've gone through this once before, you're in a better position to appreciate the value of forensic IRAC and how it can help you diagnose and redirect your analytic process.

B.   USING YOUR BASELINE

As a re-taker, your situation is unique because you have a "baseline." This means that you have some idea of your strengths and weaknesses in the Multistate subjects and the essays in terms of hard, real numbers. While you might wish that you didn't have the experience it took to acquire a baseline, you're going to make the best of the situation by using it to your advantage.

First, you're going to make every effort to get your hands on your essays. Some jurisdictions make them available to the re-taker. The availability of such materials is typically included in your application for re-examination. But since the application arrives with the failure notification, it's easy to overlook in the misery of the moment. Still, you must be strong and read through all the materials sent to you by your state's bar examiners and see if they make copies of your own essay answers available. In addition to making your own essay answers available for purchase at a small fee, some jurisdictions allow you to purchase the test questions and the selected sample answers. If they do, order them immediately. If no mention is made of this option either in the application papers or on the web site, you must contact their office immediately and inquire directly. You must not lose this opportunity because once you have your hands on your essays, you can immediately apply the IRAC self-diagnostic. This gives your study program a dramatic shot forward and it's what you need at this point.

Next, you're going to see if you can have your MBE answer sheet re-scored by hand. This information may be available from your local jurisdiction, or contact the National Conference of Bar Examiners. The answer sheets are scored electronically and I don't know about you, but I don't trust machines to always do the right thing. Maybe the machine counted an erasure instead of your correct answer choice. Don't take any chances when there exists a single possibility that you can avoid doing this again. However, you must be realistic. If your MBE score was very low and there's no way a couple of correct answer choices would make a difference between passing and failing, then you can't expect miracles. Face the facts, harden your resolve, and move on.

C. ADOPT   A   TWO–PRONGED APPROACH

Once again, because you're a re-taker, your preparation will follow a different course than a first time test-taker. You must keep two objectives in mind as your prepare: first, to preserve the general knowledge base you acquired as a result of your earlier studies; and second, to increase your mastery of the specific subjects and sections of the bar exam that caused you difficulty.

1. Preserving your general knowledge.

Let's face it: while you're likely to have retained quite a bit, it won't be nearly enough. The bar exam tests the kind of details that don't stay in the memory banks for too long. Therefore, you'll need to make a complete review of all subjects. There are a couple of ways you can proceed to ensure that you cover all the material that's going to be tested.

a. *Consider re-taking a bar review course*

Depending on your finances and whether you have the self-discipline to stick to a schedule on your own, you may want to consider re-taking a bar review course. Sometimes they have special rates for re-takers, so check first before you make any commitments.

b.   Do it on your own if you're disciplined

On the other hand, if you're a conscientious worker, you can follow the sequencing of topics covered in a bar review course on your own. Simply review your notes from the course you took previously, and follow the lectures, day by day. This will ensure that you cover all the material once again. Of course, I'm making the assumption that you've kept your bar review materials. If not, get in touch with a law school buddy and see if you can borrow them.

2.   Increasing your mastery of individual subjects and sections

By taking a targeted approach to the topics and areas of the bar exam that caused you difficulty as indicated by your scores, you can concentrate your efforts where they're needed most and where they're likely to do the most good.

a.   On the essays

As I indicated earlier in the section on bar exam essays, this portion of the bar exam represents your greatest opportunity to affect your score. But you must know how to seize that opportunity.

First, when you review your essay scores, look for any significant differences between the individual essays. If you find a range of scores, including some rather high scores, then your problem is most likely a function of the subject matter and not your general essay writing skills. You need to concentrate on learning the substantive law in the low-scoring areas and practice the technique for constructing solid statements of the law. Write sample answers and lean heavily on the "building block" approach by incorporating elements, definitions, exceptions, or distinctions, into your articulation of the rule.

On the other hand, if your scores tend to be consistent, then you need to focus on both substance and form. Work through the essay section carefully and use the forensic self-diagnostic to evaluate your essays. You should work on improving your performance on each part of an essay, beginning with articulation of the issue. Whether your jurisdiction follows the New York or New Jersey essay model, your ability to find the issue and organize your response to address that issue will make all the difference.

b.   *On the individual MBE subjects*

When you receive your MBE results, it will include a subject by subject breakdown of your scores. Because each jurisdiction determines the weight it will accord the MBE portion of the bar exam, you'll want to look at the "raw" scores and not the scaled scores. The raw score represents the actual number of correct answers. For example, if you got a raw score of "18" in Criminal Law, this means that out of the 33 possible Criminal Law questions, you got slightly more than 50% correct. If you can add but two or three more correct answers, your raw score will increase a bit, but your scaled score will jump. Because of each jurisdiction's individual scaling system, numbers do not have the usual one-to-one relationship. This means that one right answer can be worth more than one point.

Once again, all this means is that you don't have to have a perfect score to pass the bar exam. But you do need to rack up enough points. By now you surely know yourself well enough to know where the possibility for more points exist.

First, just as I suggested you do when reviewing your essay scores, you're going to look for any significant differences between individual subjects. If the numbers are consistent, then you may have a reading comprehension problem in addition to a gap in substantive knowledge. You'll want to drill yourself on reading the questions and focusing on the Bar Examiners' very particular use of vocabulary. Your ability to identify signal words and legally significant phrases will help to compensate for some reading deficiencies.

On the other hand, if there's a wide variation in scores between subjects, then it's not likely to be a reading comprehension problem, but a true subject-specific deficiency. In this case, you have to make some tough decisions. As we've seen, some subjects are easier to master than others. Pick your subjects and focus on increasing your score in the areas where you're most likely to have success. In addition to the subjects for which you have the greatest affection (if that's true of any of the subjects at this point!), I'd suggest that you hone in on those topics which feature a more direct application of rule to fact, such as Torts, Criminal Law, and Constitutional Law. Then you must buckle down and practice, practice, practice.

c. *On the MPT*

Typically, a low score on the MPT results from a lack of practice. The MPT is not difficult "legally" but is a race against the clock. Sufficient practice is an absolute necessity to master this section of the bar exam. Your goal is to make your approach to the material so mechanical that come test day, it's pure routine.

The typical errors on the MPT are two-fold: the failure to produce a working outline after concluding a read-through of the Library and the inclusion of endless background material which merely repeats the facts in the file and long, quoted passages from the cases instead of substance and analysis that addresses the issue.

If you have the opportunity to review your MPT response, then look to see whether you included unnecessary background facts before finally getting to the issue. This just takes up your valuable time without adding any point-worthy material. Instead, practice beginning your response with a direct reference to the issue you're asked to resolve.

Your goal is to practice as many MPTs as you possibly can to improve your timing and organization. Follow the blueprint and practice the technique until it becomes so mechanical that you don't have to think about it but proceed automatically.

CHAPTER 9

SOME PARTING WORDS

Hopefully, this discussion has demystified the bar exam for you and at the same time provided you with a solid work plan to follow as you prepare. As in any venture, the key to success is planning and practice. If you follow the advice and strategies offered in this book, seize the opportunity to practice from previous exams, and take advantage of the guidance your own jurisdiction provides, you'll be in a most favorable position on test day.

Good luck on the bar exam and in your future endeavors as a practicing attorney.

†